THE TRUTH AND MEANING
OF HUMAN SEXUALITY

Guidelines for Education within the Family

Publication No. 5-090
United States Catholic Conference
Washington, D.C.
ISBN 1-57455-090-X

Text and format from
LIBRERIA EDITRICE VATICANA
Vatican City

Published in the United States, February 1996

CONTENTS

V. PATHS OF FORMATION WITHIN THE FAMILY

VI. LEARNING STAGES

VII. PRACTICAL GUIDELINES

VIII. CONCLUSION

INTRODUCTION

The Situation and the Problem

1.   Among the many difficulties parents encounter today, despite different social contexts, one certainly stands out: giving children an adequate preparation for adult life, particularly with regard to education in the true meaning of sexuality. There are many reasons for this difficulty and not all of them are new.

In the past, even when the family did not provide specific sexual education, the general culture was permeated by respect for fundamental values and hence served to protect and maintain them. In the greater part of society, both in developed and developing countries, the decline of traditional models has left children deprived of consistent and positive guidance, while parents find themselves unprepared to provide adequate answers. This new context is made worse by what we observe: an eclipse of the truth about man which, among other things, exerts pressure to reduce sex to something commonplace. In this area, society and the mass media most of the time provide depersonalized, recreational and often pessimistic information. Moreover, this information does not take into account the different stages of formation and development of children and young people, and it is influenced by a distorted individualistic concept of freedom, in an ambience lacking the basic values of life, human love and the family.

Then the school, making itself available to carry out programmes of sex education, has often done this by taking the place of the family and, most of the time, with the aim of only providing information. Sometimes this really leads to the deformation of consciences. In many cases parents have given up their duty in this field or agreed to delegate it to others, because of the difficulty and their own lack of preparation.

In such a situation, many Catholic parents turn to the Church to take up the task of providing guidance and suggestions for educating their children, especially in the phase of childhood and adolescence. At times, parents themselves have brought up their difficulties when they are confronted by teaching given at school and thus brought into the home by their children. The Pontifical Council for the Family has received repeated and pressing requests to provide guidelines in support of parents in this delicate area of education.

2.   Aware of this family dimension of education for love and for living one's own sexuality properly and conscious of the unique "experience of humanity" of the

3

community of believers, our Council wishes to put forward pastoral guidelines, draw
ing on the wisdom which comes from the Word of the Lord and the values which il
luminate the teaching of the Church.

Therefore, above all, we wish to tie this help for parents to fundamental conten
about the truth and meaning of sex, within the framework of a genuine and ricl
anthropology. In offering this truth, we are aware that "every one who is of th
truth" (*John* 18: 37) hears the word of the One who is the Truth in Person (cf. *Joh*
14: 6).

This guide is meant to be neither a treatise of moral theology nor a compendiun
of psychology. But it does owe much to the gains of science, to the socio-cultura
conditions of the family, and to the proclamation of gospel values which are alway
new and can be incarnated in a concrete way in every age.

3.   In this field, the Church is strengthened by some unquestionable certainties tha
have also guided the preparation of this document.

Love is a gift of God, nourished by and expressed in the encounter of man anc
woman. Love is thus a positive force directed towards their growth in maturity a
persons. In the plan of life which represents each person's vocation, love is also ;
precious source for the self-giving which all men and women are called to make fo
their own self-realization and happiness. In fact, man is called to love as an incarnate
spirit, that is soul and body in the unity of the person. Human love hence embrace:
the body, and the body also expresses spiritual love.[1] Therefore, sexuality is no
something purely biological, rather it concerns the intimate nucleus of the person
The use of sexuality as physical giving has its own truth and reaches its full meaning
when it expresses the personal giving of man and woman even unto death. As witl
the whole of the person's life, love is exposed to the frailty brought about by origina
sin, a frailty experienced today in many socio-cultural contexts marked by strong ne
gative influences, at times deviant and traumatic. Nevertheless, the Lord's Redemp
tion has made the positive practice of chastity into something that is really possibl
and a motive for joy, both for those who have the vocation to marriage (before, ir
the time of preparation, and afterwards, in the course of married life) as well as fo
those who have the gift of a special calling to the consecrated life.

4.   In the light of the Redemption and how adolescents and young people ar
formed, the virtue of chastity is found within temperance — a cardinal virtue ele
vated and enriched by grace in baptism. So chastity is not to be understood as a re
pressive attitude. On the contrary, chastity should be understood rather as the purity

---

[1] Cf. John Paul II, Apostolic Exhortation, *Familiaris Consortio*, November 22, 1981, 21; *AAS* 74 (1982)
p. 105.

and temporary stewardship of a precious and rich gift of love, in view of the self-giving realized in each person's specific vocation. Chastity is thus that "spiritual energy capable of defending love from the perils of selfishness and aggressiveness, and able to advance it towards its full realization".[2]

The *Catechism of the Catholic Church* describes and in a sense defines chastity in this way: "Chastity means the successful integration of sexuality within the person and thus the inner unity of man in his bodily and spiritual being".[3]

5. In the framework of educating the young person for self-realization and self-giving, formation for chastity implies the collaboration first and foremost of the parents, as is the case with formation for the other virtues such as temperance, fortitude and prudence. Chastity cannot exist as a virtue without the capacity to renounce self, to make sacrifices and to wait.

In giving life, parents cooperate with the creative power of God and receive the gift of a new responsibility — not only to feed their children and satisfy their material and cultural needs, but above all to pass on to them the lived truth of the faith and to educate them in love of God and neighbour. This is the parents' first duty in the heart of the "domestic church".[4]

The Church has always affirmed that parents have the duty and the right to be the first and the principal educators of their children.

Taking up the teaching of the Second Vatican Council, the *Catechism of the Catholic Church* says: "It is imperative to give suitable and timely instruction to young people, above all in the heart of their own families, about the dignity of married love, its role and its exercise".[5]

6. The challenges raised today by the mentality and social environment should not discourage parents. In fact it is worth recalling that Christians have had to face up to similar challenges of materialistic hedonism from the time of the first evangelization. Moreover, "This kind of critical reflection should lead our society, which certainly contains many positive aspects on the material and cultural level, to realize that, from various points of view, it is a *society which is sick* and is creating profound distortions in man. Why is this happening? The reason is that our society has broken away from the full truth about man, from the truth about what man and woman really are as persons. Thus it cannot adequately comprehend the real meaning of the gift of persons in marriage, responsible love at the service of fatherhood and motherhood, and the true grandeur of procreation and education".[6]

---

[2] *Ibid.*, 33.

[3] *Catechism of the Catholic Church*, October 11, 1992, 2337.

[4] Cf. Second Vatican Council, Dogmatic Constitution on the Church, *Lumen Gentium*, 11; Decree on the Apostolate of the Laity, *Apostolicam Actuositatem*, 11.

[5] *Catechism of the Catholic Church*, 1632, citing Vatican Council II, Pastoral Constitution on the Church in the Modern World, *Gaudium et Spes*, 49.

[6] John Paul II, Letter to Families, *Gratissimam sane*, February 2, 1994, 20: *AAS* 86 (1994), p. 917.

7.   Therefore, the educative work of parents is indispensable for, "If it is true that by giving life *parents* share in God's creative work, it is also true that by raising their children they *become sharers in his paternal and at the same time maternal way of teaching......Through Christ* all education, within the family, and outside of it, *becomes part of God's own saving pedagogy,* which is addressed to individuals and families and culminates in the Paschal Mystery of the Lord's Death and Resurrection".[7]

In their at times delicate and arduous task, parents must not let themselves become discouraged, rather they should place their trust in the help of God the Creator and Christ the Redeemer. They should remember that the Church prays for them with the words that Pope Saint Clement I raised to the Lord for all who bear authority in his name: "Grant to them, Lord, health, peace, concord and stability, so that they may exercise without offence the sovereignty that you have given them. Master, heavenly King of the ages, you give glory, honour and power over the things of the earth to the sons of men. Direct, Lord, their counsel, following what is pleasing and acceptable in your sight, so that by exercising with devotion and in peace and gentleness the power that you have given to them, they may find favour with you".[8]

On the other hand, having given and welcomed life in an atmosphere of love, parents are rich in an educative potential which no one else possesses. In a unique way they know their own children; they know them in their unrepeatable identity and by experience they possess the secrets and the resources of true love.

---

[7] *Ibid.,* 16.
[8] Saint Clement of Rome, *Letter to the Corinthians,* 61: 1-2; cf. *Catechism of the Catholic Church,* 1900.

I

CALLED TO TRUE LOVE

8. *As the image of God, man is created for love.* This truth was fully revealed to us in the New Testament, together with the mystery of the inner life of the Trinity: "God is love (*1 John* 4: 8) and in himself he lives a mystery of personal loving communion. Creating the human race in his own image... God inscribed in the humanity of man and woman the vocation, and thus the capacity and responsibility, of love and communion. Love is therefore the fundamental and innate vocation of every human being".[9] The whole meaning of true freedom, and self-control which follows from it, is thus directed towards self-giving in communion and friendship with God and with others.[10]

Human Love as Self-Giving

9. The person is thus capable of a higher kind of love than concupiscence, which only sees objects as a means to satisfy one's appetites; the person is capable rather of friendship and self-giving, with the capacity to recognize and love persons for themselves. Like the love of God, this is a love capable of generosity. One desires the good of the other because he or she is recognized as worthy of being loved. This is a love which generates communion between persons, because each considers the good of the other as his or her own good. This is a self-giving made to one who loves us, a self-giving whose inherent goodness is discovered and activated in the communion of persons and where one learns the value of loving and of being loved.

Each person is called to love as friendship and self-giving. Each person is freed from the tendency to selfishness by the love of others, in the first place by parents or those who take their place and, definitively, by God, from whom all true love proceeds and in whose love alone does man discover to what extent he is loved. Here we find the root of the educative power of Christianity: "*Humanity is loved by God!* This very simple yet profound proclamation is owed to humanity by the

---

[9] *Familiaris Consortio,* 11.

[10] Cf. John Paul II, Apostolic Letter, *Mulieris Dignitatem,* August 15, 1988, 7 and 18; *AAS* 80 (1988), pp. 1667 and 1693.

Church".[11] In this way Christ has revealed his true identity to man: "Christ the new Adam, in the very revelation of the mystery of the Father and of his love, fully reveals man to himself and brings to light his most high calling".[12]

The love revealed by Christ "which the Apostle Paul celebrates in the First Letter to the Corinthians...is certainly *a demanding love*. But this is precisely the source of its beauty: by the very fact that it is demanding, it builds up the true good of man and allows it to radiate to others".[13] Therefore it is a love which respects and builds up the person because "Love is true when *it creates the good of persons and of communities; it creates that good and gives it to others*".[14]

Love and Human Sexuality

10.   Man is called to love and to self-giving in the unity of body and spirit. Femininity and masculinity are complementary gifts, through which human sexuality is an integrating part of the concrete capacity for love which God has inscribed in man and woman. "Sexuality is a fundamental component of personality, one of its modes of being, of manifestation, of communicating with others, of feeling, of expressing and of living human love".[15] This capacity for love as self-giving is thus "incarnated" in the *nuptial meaning of the body,* which bears the imprint of the person's masculinity and femininity. "The human body, with its sex, and its masculinity and femininity, seen in the very mystery of creation, is not only a source of fruitfulness and procreation, as in the whole natural order, but includes right 'from the beginning' the 'nuptial' attribute, that is, *the capacity of expressing love: that love precisely in which the man-person becomes a gift* and — by means of this gift — fulfils the very meaning of his being and existence".[16] Every form of love will always bear this masculine and feminine character.

11.   *Human sexuality is thus a good,* part of that created gift which God saw as being "very good", when he created the human person in his image and likeness, and "male and female he created them" (*Genesis* 1:27). Insofar as it is a way of relating and being open to others, sexuality has love as its intrinsic end, more precisely, love as donation and acceptance, love as giving and receiving. The relationship between a

---

[11] John Paul II, Apostolic Exhortation, *Christifideles Laici,* December 30 1988, 34; *AAS* 81 (1989), p. 456.

[12] *Gaudium et Spes,* 22.

[13] Letter to Families, *Gratissimam Sane,* 14.

[14] *Ibid.,* 14.

[15] Congregation for Catholic Education, *Educational Guidance in Human Love,* November 1, 1983, 4; *L'Osservatore Romano,* English edition, December 5, 1983, p. 5.

[16] John Paul II, General Audience, January 16, 1980, 1; *L'Osservatore Romano,* English edition, January 21, 1983, p. 1.

man and a woman is essentially a relationship of love: "Sexuality, oriented, elevated and integrated by love acquires truly human quality".[17] When such love exists in marriage, self-giving expresses, through the body, the complementarity and totality of the gift. Married love thus becomes a power which enriches persons and makes them grow and, at the same time, it contributes to building up the civilization of love. But when the sense and meaning of gift is lacking in sexuality, a "civilization of things and not of persons" takes over, "a civilization in which persons are used in the same way as things are used. In the context of a civilization of use, woman can become an object for man, children a hindrance to parents...".[18]

12.   *The gift of God:* this great truth and basic fact stands at the centre of the Christian conscience of parents and their children. Here we refer to the gift which God has given us in calling us to life, to exist as man or woman in an unrepeatable existence, full of endless possibilities for growing spiritually and morally: *"human life is a gift received in order then to be given as a gift".*[19] "In fact the gift reveals, so to speak, a particular characteristic of human existence, or rather, of the very essence of the person. When God Yahweh says that 'it is not good that man should be alone' (*Genesis* 2:18), he affirms that 'alone', man does not completely realize his existence. He realizes it only by existing *'with some one'* — and even more deeply and completely: by existing *'for some one'".*[20] Married love is fulfilled in openness to the other person and in self-giving, taking the form of a total gift that belongs to this state of life. Moreover, the vocation to the consecrated life always finds its meaning in self-giving, sustained by a special grace, the gift of oneself "to God alone with an undivided heart in a remarkable manner"[21] in order to serve him more fully in the Church. Therefore, in every condition and state of life, this gift comes to be ever more wondrous by redeeming grace, through which we become "partakers of the divine nature" (*2 Peter* 1:4) and are called to live the supernatural communion of love together with God and with our brothers and sisters. Even in the most delicate situations, Christian parents cannot forget that the gift of God is there, at the very basis of all personal and family history.

13.   "As an incarnate spirit, that is, a soul which expresses itself in a body and a body informed by an immortal spirit, man is called to love in his unified totality. Love includes the human body, and the body is made a sharer in spiritual love".[22] The

---

[17] *Educational Guidance in Human Love,* 6.

[18] Letter to Families, *Gratissimam Sane,* 13.

[19] John Paul II, Encyclical Letter, *Evangelium Vitae,* March 25, 1995, 92; *AAS* (1995), p. 506

[20] John Paul II, General Audience, January 9, 1980, 2; *L'Osservatore Romano,* English edition, January 14, 1989, p. 1.

[21] *Catechism of the Catholic Church,* 2349.

[22] *Familiaris Consortio,* 11.

meaning of sexuality itself is to be understood in the light of Christian Revelation: "Sexuality characterizes man and woman not only on the physical level, but also on the psychological and spiritual, making its mark on each of their expressions. Such diversity, linked to the complementarity of the two sexes, allows thorough response to the design of God according to the vocation to which each one is called".[23]

Married Love

14. When love is lived out in marriage, it includes and surpasses friendship. Love between a man and woman is achieved when they give themselves totally, each in turn according to their own masculinity and femininity, founding on the marriage covenant that communion of persons where God has willed that human life be conceived, grow and develop. To this married love, and to this love alone, belongs sexual giving, "realized in a truly human way only if it is an integral part of the love by which a man and a woman commit themselves totally to one another until death".[24] The *Catechism of the Catholic Church* recalls: "In marriage the physical intimacy of the spouses becomes a sign and pledge of spiritual communion. Marriage bonds between baptized persons are sanctified by the sacrament".[25]

Love Open to Life

15. The revealing sign of authentic married love is openness to life: "In its most profound reality, love is essentially a gift; and conjugal love, while leading the spouses to the reciprocal 'knowledge'....does not end with the couple, because it makes them capable of the greatest possible gift, the gift by which they become cooperators with God for giving life to a new human person. Thus the couple, while giving themselves to one another, give not just themselves but also the reality of children, who are a living reflection of their love, a permanent sign of conjugal unity and a living and inseparable synthesis of their being a father and a mother".[26] From this communion of love and life spouses draw that human and spiritual richness and that positive atmosphere for offering their children the support of education for love and chastity.

[23] *Educational Guidance in Human Love*, 5.
[24] *Familiaris Consortio*, 11.
[25] *Catechism of the Catholic Church*, 2360.
[26] *Familiaris Consortio*, 14.

II

TRUE LOVE AND CHASTITY

16.   As we will later observe, virginal and married love are the two forms in which the person's call to love is fulfilled. In order for both to develop, they require the commitment to live chastity, in conformity with each person's own state of life. As the *Catechism of the Catholic Church* says, sexuality "becomes personal and truly human when it is integrated into the relationship of one person to another, in the complete and mutual lifelong gift of a man and a woman".[27] Insofar as it entails sincere self-giving, it is obvious that growth in love is helped by that discipline of the feelings, passions and emotions which leads us to self-mastery. One cannot give what one does not possess. If the person is not master of self — through the virtues and, in a concrete way, through chastity — he or she lacks that self-possession which makes self-giving possible. *Chastity is the spiritual power which frees love from selfishness and aggression.* To the degree that a person weakens chastity, his or her love becomes more and more selfish, that is, satisfying a desire for pleasure and no longer self-giving.

Chastity as Self-Giving

17.   Chastity is the joyous affirmation of someone who knows how to live self-giving, free from any form of self-centred slavery. This presupposes that the person has learnt how to accept other people, to relate with them, while respecting their dignity in diversity. The chaste person is not self-centred, not involved in selfish relationships with other people. Chastity makes the personality harmonious. It matures it and fills it with inner peace. This purity of mind and body helps develop true self-respect and at the same time makes one capable of respecting others, because it makes one see in them persons to reverence, insofar as they are created in the image of God and through grace are children of God, re-created by Christ who "called you out of darkness into his marvellous light" (*1 Peter* 2:9).

Self-Mastery

18.   "Chastity includes an *apprenticeship in self-mastery* which is a training in human freedom. The alternative is clear: either man governs his passions and finds peace, or

---

[27] *Catechism of the Catholic Church,* 2337.

he lets himself be dominated by them and becomes unhappy".[28] Every person knows, by experience, that chastity requires rejecting certain thoughts, words and sinful actions, as Saint Paul was careful to clarify and point out (cf. *Romans* 1:18; 6: 12-14; 1 *Corinthians* 6: 9-11; *2 Corinthians* 7: 1; *Galatians* 5: 16-23; *Ephesians* 4: 17-24; 5: 3-13; *Colossians* 3: 5-8; *1 Thessalonians* 4: 1-18; *1 Timothy* 1: 8-11; 4: 12). To achieve this requires ability and an *attitude of self-mastery* which are signs of inner freedom, of responsibility towards oneself and others. At the same time, these signs bear witness to a faithful conscience. Such self-mastery involves both avoiding occasions which might provoke or encourage sin as well as knowing how to overcome one's own natural instinctive impulses.

19.   When the family is providing real educational support and encouraging the exercise of all the virtues, education for chastity is made easy and lacks *inner conflicts,* even if at certain times young people can experience particularly delicate situations. For some who find themselves in situations where chastity is offended against and not valued, living in a chaste way can demand a hard or even a heroic struggle. Nonetheless, with the grace of Christ, flowing from his spousal love for the Church, everyone can live chastely even if they find themselves in unfavourable circumstances.

The very fact that all are called to holiness, as the Second Vatican Council teaches, makes it easier to understand that everyone can be in situations where heroic acts of virtue are indispensable, whether in celibate life or marriage, and that in fact in one way or another this happens to everyone for shorter or longer periods of time.[29] Therefore, married life also entails a joyous and demanding path to holiness.

Chastity in Marriage

20.   "Married people are called to live conjugal chastity; others practise chastity in continence".[30] Parents are well aware that *living conjugal chastity themselves* is the most valid premise for educating their children in chaste love and in holiness of life. This means that parents should be aware that God's love is present in their love, and hence that their sexual giving should also be lived out in respect for God and for his plan of love, with fidelity, honour and generosity towards one's spouse and towards the life which can arise from their act of love. Only in this way can their love be an

---

[28] *Ibid.,* 2339.

[29] Cf. John Paul II, Address to the Participants at the Study Seminar on "Responsible Parenthood", organised by the University of the Sacred Heart and the John Paul II Institute, September 17, 1983; *L'Osservatore Romano*, English edition, October 10, 1983, pp. 7 and 16.

[30] *Catechism of the Catholic Church*, 2349.

expression of *charity*.[31] Therefore, in marriage Christians are called to live this self-giving in a right personal relationship with God. This relationship is thus an expression of their faith and love for God with the fidelity and generous fruitfulness which distinguishes divine love.[32] Only in this way do they respond to the love of God and fulfil his will, which the Commandments help us to know. There is no legitimate love, at its highest level, which is not also love for God. To love the Lord implies responding positively to his commandments: "If you love me, you will keep my commandments" (*John* 14:15).[33]

21.   In order to live chastely, man and woman need the continuous illumination of the Holy Spirit. "At the centre of the spirituality of marriage...lies chastity, not only as a moral virtue (formed by love), but likewise as a virtue connected with the gifts of the Holy Spirit — *above all the gift of respect for what comes from God (donum pietatis)*... So therefore, the interior order of married life, which enables the 'manifestations of affection' to develop according to their right proportion and meaning, is a fruit not only *of the virtue* which the couple practise, but also *of the gifts* of the Holy Spirit *with which they cooperate*".[34]

On the other hand, convinced that their own chaste life and the daily effort of bearing witness are the premise and condition for their educational task, parents should also consider any attack on the virtue and chastity of their children as an *offence against the life of faith itself that threatens and impoverishes their own communion of life and grace* (cf. *Ephesians* 6:12).

Education for Chastity

22.   Educating children for chastity strives to achieve three objectives: (a) to maintain in the family *a positive atmosphere of love, virtue and respect for the gifts of God*, in particular the gift of life; [35] (a) to help children to understand the value of sexuality and chastity in stages, sustaining their growth through enlightening word, ex-

---

[31] See below n. 54.

[32] Cf. Paul VI, Encyclical Letter, *Humanae Vitae*, July 28, 1968, 8 and 9; *AAS* 60 (1968), pp. 485-486.

[33] Not to do so is always self-delusion, as Saint John of Avila observes: some people are so clouded in their minds that "they believe that if their heart moves them to do anything, they must do it, even if it is against the commandments of God. They say that they love Him so much that if they break his commandments they do not lose his love. In this way they forget that the Son of God preached the contrary from his own lips: *whoever welcomes my commandments and observes them, this man loves me* (John 14:21); *if anyone loves me he will keep my commandments* (John 14:23). And *anyone who does not love me does not keep my words.* Thus he makes us understand clearly that whoever does not keep his words has neither his friendship nor his love. As Saint Augustine says: 'no-one can love the king if he abhorrs his commandments'." *Audi filia*, c. 50.

[34] John Paul II, General Audience, November 14, 1984, 2; *L'Osservatore Romano*, English Edition, November 19, 1984, p. 1.

[35] Cf. *Evangelium Vitae*, 97.

ample and prayer; (c) to help them understand and discover *their own vocation to marriage or to consecrated virginity for the sake of the Kingdom of Heaven* in harmony with and respecting their attitudes and inclinations and the gifts of the Spirit.

23.   Other educators can assist in this task, but they can only take the place of parents for serious reasons of physical or moral incapacity. On this point the Magisterium of the Church has expressed itself clearly,[36] in relation to the whole educative process of children: "The role of parents in education is of such importance that it is almost impossible to find an adequate substitute. It is therefore the duty of parents to create a family atmosphere inspired by love and devotion to God and their fellow-men which will promote an integrated, personal and social education of their children. The family is therefore the principal school of the social virtues which are necessary to every society".[37] In fact education is the parents' domain insofar as their educational task continues the generation of life; moreover, it is an *offering of their humanity*[38] to their children to which they are solemnly bound in the very moment of celebrating their marriage. "*Parents* are the *first and most important educators* of their children, and they also possess a *fundamental competency* in this area: they are *educators because they are parents.* They share their individual mission with other individuals or institutions, such as the Church and the State. But the mission of education must always be carried out in accordance with a proper application of the *principle of subsidiarity.* This implies the legitimacy and indeed the need of giving assistance to the parents, but finds its intrinsic and absolute limit in their prevailing right and their actual capabilities. The principle of subsidiarity is thus at the service of parental love, meeting the good of the family unit. For parents by themselves are not capable of satisfying every requirement of the whole process of raising children, especially in matters concerning their schooling and the entire gamut of socialization. Subsidiarity thus complements paternal and maternal love and confirms its fundamental nature, inasmuch as all other participants in the process of education are only able to carry out their responsibilities *in the name of the parents, with their consent* and, to a certain degree, *with their authorization*".[39]

24.   In particular, the project of education in sexuality and true love, open to self-giving, is confronted today by a culture guided by positivism, as the Holy Father notes in the *Letter to Families:* "..the development of contemporary civilization is linked to a scientific and technological progress which is often achieved in a one-sided way, and thus appears purely positivistic. Positivism, as we know, results in ag-

---

[36] Cf. *Familiaris Consortio,* 36-37.
[37] Vatican Council II, Declaration on Christian Education, *Gravissimum Educationis,* 3.
[38] Letter to Families, *Gratissimam sane,* 16.
[39] *Ibid.,* 16.

nosticism in theory and utilitarianism in practice and in ethics... *Utilitarianism* is a civilization of production and of use, a civilization of things and not of persons, a civilization in which persons are used in the same way as things are used... To be convinced that this is the case, one need only to look at *certain sexual education programmes* introduced into the schools, often notwithstanding the disagreement and even the protests of many parents...".[40]

In this context, based on the teaching of the Church and with her support, parents must reclaim their own task. By associating together, wherever this is necessary or useful, they should put into action an educational project marked by the true values of the person and Christian love and taking a clear position that surpasses ethical utilitarianism. For education to correspond to the objective needs of true love, parents should provide this education within their own autonomous responsibility.

25. Moreover, in relation to preparation for marriage the teaching of the Church states that the family must remain the main protagonist in this educational work.[41]

Certainly "the changes that have taken place within almost all modern societies demand that not only the family but also society and the Church should be involved in the effort of properly preparing young people for their future responsibilities".[42] It is precisely with this end in view that the educational task of the family takes on greater importance from the earliest years: "Remote preparation begins in early childhood in that wise family training which leads children to discover themselves as being endowed with a rich and complex psychology and with a particular personality with its own strengths and weaknesses".[43]

---

[40] *Ibid.*, 13.
[41] Cf. *Familiaris Consortio*, 66.
[42] *Ibid., loc. cit.*.
[43] *Ibid., loc. cit.*

III

IN THE LIGHT OF VOCATION

26.   The family carries out *a decisive role* in cultivating and developing all vocations, as the Second Vatican Council taught: "From the marriage of Christians there comes the family in which new citizens of human society are born and, by the grace of the Holy Spirit in Baptism, those are made children of God so that the People of God may be perpetuated throughout the centuries. In what might be regarded as the domestic church, the parents by word and example, are the first heralds of the faith with regard to their children. They must foster the vocation which is proper to each child, and this with special care if it be to religion".[44] Yet the very fact that vocations flourish is the sign of adequate pastoral care of the family: "where there is an effective and enlightened *family apostolate,* just as it becomes normal to accept life as a gift from God, so it is easier for God's voice to resound and to find a more generous hearing".[45]

Here we are dealing with vocations to marriage or to virginity or celibacy, but these are always vocations to holiness. Indeed, the document *Lumen Gentium* presents the Second Vatican Council's teaching on *the universal call to holiness:* "Strengthened by so many and such great means of salvation, all the faithful, whatever their condition or state — though each in his own way — are called by the Lord to that perfection of sanctity by which the Father himself is perfect".[46]

1. The Vocation to Marriage

27.   Formation for true love is always the best preparation for the vocation to marriage. In the family, children and young people can learn to live human sexuality within the solid context of Christian life. They can gradually discover that a stable Christian marriage cannot be regarded as a matter of convenience or mere sexual attraction. By the fact that it is a vocation, marriage must involve a carefully considered choice, a mutual commitment before God and the constant seeking of his help in prayer.

---

[44] *Lumen Gentium,* 11.

[45] John Paul II, Address to the Sixteenth General Assembly of the Italian Episcopal Conference, May 15, 1979, 4; *L'Osservatore Romano,* English edition, June 11, 1979, p. 14.

[46] *Lumen Gentium,* 11.

28.   Committed to the task of educating their children for love, Christian parents first of all can take awareness of their married love as a reference point. As the Encyclical *Humanae Vitae* states, such love "reveals its true nature and nobility when it is considered in its supreme origin, God, who is love (cf. *1 John* 4: 8), 'the Father from whom every family in heaven and on earth is named' (*Ephesians* 3: 15). Marriage is not, then, the effect of chance or the product of evolution of unconscious natural forces; it is the wise institution of the Creator to realize in mankind his design of love. By means of the reciprocal personal gift of self, proper and exclusive to them, husband and wife tend towards the communion of their beings in view of mutual personal perfection, to collaborate with God in the generation and education of new lives. For baptized persons, moreover, marriage invests the dignity of a sacramental sign of grace, inasmuch as it represents the union of Christ and of the Church".[47]

The Holy Father's *Letter to Families* recalls that: "The family is in fact a community of persons whose proper way of existing and living together is communion: *communio personarum*".[48] Going back to the teaching of the Second Vatican Council, the Holy Father teaches that such a communion involves "a certain similarity between the union of the divine Persons and union of God's children in truth and love".[49] "This rich and meaningful formulation first of all confirms what is central to the identity of every man and every woman. This identity consists in the *capacity to live in truth and love;* even more, it consists in the need of truth and love as an essential dimension of the life of the person. Man's need for truth and love opens him both to God and to creatures: it opens him to other people, to life in communion, and in particular to marriage and to the family".[50]

29.   As the Encyclical *Humanae Vitae* affirms, married love has *four characteristics:* it is *human* love (physical and spiritual), it is *total, faithful and fruitful* love.[51]

These characteristics are founded on the fact that "In marriage man and woman are so firmly united as to become, to use the words of the Book of Genesis — one flesh (*Genesis* 2:24). Male and female in their physical constitution, the two human subjects, even though physically different, *share equally in the capacity to live in truth and love.* This capacity, characteristic of the human being as a person, has at the same time both a spiritual and a bodily dimension... The family which results from this

---

[47] *Humanae Vitae,* 8.
[48] Letter to Families, *Gratissimam Sane,* 7.
[49] *Gaudium et Spes,* 24.
[50] Letter to Families, *Gratissimam Sane,* 8.
[51] Cf. *Humanae Vitae,* 9.

union draws its inner solidity from the covenant between the spouses, which Christ raised to a Sacrament. The family draws its proper character as a community, its traits of communion, from that fundamental communion of the spouses which is prolonged in their children. *Will you accept children lovingly from God, and bring them up according to the law of Christ and his Church?*, the celebrant asks during the Rite of Marriage. The answer given by the spouses reflects the most profound truth of the love which unites them".[52] With the same formula, spouses commit themselves and promise to be "faithful forever" [53] because their fidelity really flows from this communion of persons which is rooted in the plan of the Creator, in Trinitarian Love and in the Sacrament which expresses the faithful union between Christ and the Church.

30.   Christian marriage is a *sacrament* whereby sexuality is integrated into a path to holiness, through a bond reinforced by the indissoluble unity of the sacrament: "The gift of the sacrament is at the same time a vocation and commandment for the Christian spouses, that they may remain faithful to each other forever, beyond every trial and difficulty, in generous obedience to the holy will of the Lord: 'What therefore God has joined together, let not man put asunder' ".[54]

Parents Face a Current Concern

31.   Unfortunately, even in Christian societies today, parents have reason to be concerned about *the stability of their children's future marriages*. Nevertheless, in spite of the rising number of divorces and the growing crisis of the family, they should respond with optimism, committing themselves to give their children a deep Christian formation to make them able to overcome various difficulties. Actually, the love for chastity, which parents help to form, favours mutual respect between man and woman and provides a capacity for compassion, tolerance, generosity, and above all, a spirit of sacrifice, without which love cannot endure. Children will thus come to marriage with that realistic wisdom about which Saint Paul speaks when he teaches that husband and wife must continually give way to one another in love, cherishing one another with mutual patience and affection (cf. *1 Corinthians* 7: 3-6; *Ephesians* 5: 21-23).

32.   Through this *remote formation for chastity in the family*, adolescents and young people learn to live sexuality in its personal dimension, rejecting any kind of separation of sexuality from love — understood as self-giving — and any separation of the love between husband and wife from the family.

---

[52] Letter to Families, *Gratissimam Sane*, 8.
[53] *Rituale Romanum, Ordo celebrandi matrimonium*, 60.
[54] *Familiaris Consortio*, 20, citing Matthew 19:6.

Parental respect for life and the mystery of procreation will spare the child or young person from the false idea that the two dimensions of the conjugal act, unitive and procreative, can be separated at will. Thus the family comes to be recognized as an inseparable part of the vocation to marriage.

A Christian education for chastity within the family cannot remain silent about the moral gravity involved in separating the unitive dimension from the procreative dimension within married life. This happens above all in contraception and artificial procreation. In the first case, one intends to seek sexual pleasure, intervening in the conjugal act to avoid conception; in the second case conception is sought by substituting the conjugal act with a technique. These are actions contrary to the truth of married love and contrary to full communion between husband and wife.

Forming young people for chastity should thus become a preparation for responsible fatherhood and motherhood, which "directly concern the moment in which a man and a woman, uniting themselves in one flesh, can become parents. This is a moment of special value both for their interpersonal relationship and for their service to life: they can become parents — father and mother — by communicating life to a new human being. *The two dimensions of conjugal union,* the unitive and the procreative, *cannot be artificially separated* without damaging the deepest truth of the conjugal act itself".[55]

It is also necessary to put before young people the consequences, which are always very serious, of separating sexuality from procreation when someone reaches the stage of practising sterilization and abortion or pursuing sexual activity dissociated from married love, before and outside of marriage.

Much of the moral order and marital harmony of the family, hence also the true good of society, depends on this timely education, which finds its place in God's plan, in the very structure of sexuality and the intimate nature of marriage.

33. Parents who carry out their own right and duty to form their children for chastity can be certain that they are helping them in turn to build stable and united families, thus anticipating, insofar as this is possible, the joys of paradise: "How can I ever express the happiness of the marriage that is joined together by the Church, strengthened by an offering, sealed by a blessing, announced by angels and ratified by the Father....They are both brethren and both fellow servants; there is no separation between them in spirit or flesh....Christ rejoices in them and he sends them his peace; where the couple is, there he is also to be found, and where he is, evil can no longer abide".[56]

2. The Vocation to Virginity and Celibacy

34. Christian revelation presents the two vocations to love: *marriage and virginity.* In some societies today, not only marriage and the family, but also vocations to the

---

[55] Letter to Families, *Gratissimam Sane* 12; cf. *Humanae Vitae,* 12; *Catechism of the Catholic Church,* 2366.
[56] Cf. Tertullian, *Ad uxorem,* II, VIII, 6-8: *CCL* 1, 393-394; cf. *Familiaris Consortio,* 13.

priesthood and the religious life, are often in a state of crisis. The two situations are inseparable: "When marriage is not esteemed, neither can consecrated virginity or celibacy exist; when human sexuality is not regarded as a great value given by the Creator, the renunciation of it for the sake of the kingdom of heaven loses its meaning".[57] A lack of vocations follows from the breakdown of the family, yet where parents are generous in welcoming life, children will be more likely to be generous when it comes to the question of offering themselves to God: "Families must once again express *a generous love for life* and place themselves at its service above all by accepting the children which the Lord wants to give them with a sense of responsibility not detached from peaceful trust", and they may bring this acceptance to fulfilment not only "through a continuing educational effort but also *through an obligatory commitment,* at times perhaps neglected, to help teenagers especially and young people *to accept the vocational dimension of every living being,* within God's plan... Human life acquires fullness when it becomes a *self-gift:* a gift which can express itself in *matrimony,* in *consecrated virginity,* in *self-dedication* to one's neighbour towards an ideal, or in the *choice of priestly ministry.* Parents will truly serve the life of their children if they help them *make their own lives a gift,* respecting their mature choices and fostering joyfully each vocation, including the religious and priestly one".[58]

When he deals with sexual education in *Familiaris Consortio,* this is why Pope John Paul II affirms: "Indeed Christian parents, discerning the signs of God's call, will devote special attention and care to education in virginity or celibacy as the supreme form of that self-giving that constitutes the very meaning of human sexuality".[59]

Parents and Priestly or Religious Vocations

35.   Parents should therefore rejoice if they see in any of their children the signs of God's call to the higher vocation of virginity or celibacy for the love of the Kingdom of Heaven. They should accordingly adapt formation for chaste love to the needs of those children, encouraging them on their own path up to the time of entering the seminary or house of formation, or until this specific call to self-giving with an undivided heart matures. They must respect and appreciate the freedom of each of their children, encouraging their personal vocation and without trying to impose a predetermined vocation on them.

The Second Vatican Council clearly set out this distinct and honourable task of parents, who are supported in their work by teachers and priests: "Parents should

---

[57] *Familaris Consortio,* 16.

[58] John Paul II, Address to Participants in a Family Ministry Convention sponsored by the Italian Episcopal Conference, April 28, 1990, 3 and 4; *L'Osservatore Romano,* English edition, May 7, 1990, p. 2.

[59] *Familiaris Consortio,* 37.

nurture and protect religious vocations in their children by educating them in Christian virtues".[60] "The duty of fostering vocations falls on the whole Christian community....The greatest contribution is made by families which are animated by a spirit of faith, charity and piety and which provide, as it were, a first seminary, and by parishes in whose abundant life the young people themselves take an active part".[61] "Parents, teachers and all who are in any way concerned in the education of boys and young men ought to train them in such a way that they will know the solicitude of the Lord for his flock and be alive to the needs of the Church. In this way they will be prepared when the Lord calls to answer generously with the prophet: 'Here am I! send me' (*Isaiah* 6:8)".[62]

This necessary family context for maturing religious and priestly vocations brings to mind the serious situation of many families, especially in certain countries, families with an impoverished life because they have chosen to deprive themselves of children or where they have only one child, a situation in which it is very difficult for vocations to arise and even difficult to develop a full social education.

36.   The truly Christian family will also be able to communicate an understanding of the value of celibacy to unmarried children or those who are incapable of marriage for reasons apart from their own will. If they are formed well from childhood and during their youth, they will be equipped to face their own situation more easily. Likewise, they will be able to discover the will of God in such a situation and so find a sense of vocation and peace in their own lives.[63] These persons, especially if they have some kind of physical disability, need to be shown the great possibilities for self-realization and spiritual fruitfulness which are open to those who make a commitment to help their poorest and most needy brothers and sisters, sustained by faith and the love of God.

---

[60] Vatican Council II, Decree on the Renewal of the Religious Life, *Perfectae Caritatis*, 24.
[61] Vatican Council II, Decree on the Training of Priests, *Optatam Totius*, 2.
[62] Vatican Council II, Decree on the Ministry and Life of Priests, *Presbyterorum Ordinis*, 11.
[63] Cf. *Familiaris Consortio*, 16.

IV

FATHER AND MOTHER AS EDUCATORS

37.   In granting married persons the privilege and great responsibility of becoming parents, God gives them the grace to carry out their mission adequately. Moreover, in the task of educating their children, parents are enlightened by "two fundamental truths...: first, that man is called to live in truth and love; and second, that everyone finds fulfillment through the sincere gift of self".[64] As spouses, parents and ministers of the sacramental grace of marriage, they are sustained from day to day by special spiritual energies, received from Jesus Christ who loves and nurtures his Bride, the Church.

As husband and wife who have become "one flesh" through the bond of marriage, they share the duty to educate their children through willing collaboration nourished by vigorous mutual dialogue that "has a new specific source in the sacrament of marriage, which consecrates them for the strictly Christian education of their children: that is to say, it calls upon them to share in the very authority and love of God the Father and Christ the shepherd, and in the motherly love of the Church, and it enriches them with wisdom, counsel, fortitude and all the other gifts of the Holy Spirit in order to help the children in their growth as human beings and as Christians".[65]

38.   In the context of formation in chastity, "fatherhood-motherhood" also includes *one parent who is left alone and adoptive parents.* The task of a single parent is certainly not easy because the support of the other spouse and the role and example of a parent of the other sex is lacking. But God sustains single parents with a special love and calls them to take on this task with the same generosity and sensitivity with which they love and care for their children in other areas of family life.

39.   Some other persons are called upon in certain cases to take the place of parents: those who take on the parental role in a permanent way, for instance, for orphans or abandoned children. They, too, have the task of educating children and

---

[64] Letter to Families, *Gratissimam Sane,* 16.
[65] *Familiaris Consortio,* 38.

young people in an overall sense, as well as in chastity, and they will receive the grace of their state of life to do this according to the same principles that guide Christian parents.

40. Parents must never feel alone in this task. The Church supports and encourages them, confident that they can carry out this function better than anyone else. She also encourages those men or women who, often with great sacrifice, give children without parents a form of parental love and family life. In any case, all of them must approach this duty in a spirit of prayer, open and obedient to the moral truths of faith and reason that integrate the teaching of the Church, and always seeing children and young people as persons, children of God and heirs to the Kingdom of Heaven.

The Rights and Duties of Parents

41. Before going into the practical details of young people's formation in chastity, it is extremely important for parents to be aware of their *rights and duties,* particularly in the face of a State or a school that tends to take up the initiative in the area of sex education.

The Holy Father John Paul II reaffirms this in *Familiaris Consortio:* "The right and duty of parents to give education is *essential,* since it is connected with the transmission of human life; it is *original and primary* with regard to the educational role of others, on account of the uniqueness of the loving relationship between parents and children; and it is *irreplaceable and inalienable,* and therefore incapable of being entirely delegated to others or usurped by others",[66] except in the case, as mentioned at the beginning, of physical or psychological impossibility.

42. This doctrine is based on the teaching of the Second Vatican Council,[67] and is also proclaimed by the *Charter of the Rights of the Family:* "Since they have conferred life on their children, parents have the original, primary and inalienable right to educate them; hence they ...have the right to educate their children in conformity with their moral and religious convictions, taking into account the cultural traditions of the family which favour the good and the dignity of the child; they should also receive from society the necessary aid and assistance to perform their educational role properly".[68]

---

[66] *Familiaris Consortio,* 36
[67] Cf. *Gravissimum Educationis,* 3.
[68] *Charter of the Rights of the Family,* presented by the Holy See, October 22, 1983, Article 5.

43. The Pope insists upon the fact that this holds especially with regard to sexuality: "Sex education, which is a basic right and duty of parents, must always be carried out under their attentive guidance, whether at home or in educational centres chosen and controlled by them. In this regard, the Church reaffirms the law of subsidiarity, which the school is bound to observe when it cooperates in sex education, by entering into the same spirit that animates the parents".[69]

The Holy Father adds, "In view of the close links between the sexual dimension of the person and his or her ethical values, education must bring the children to a knowledge of and respect for the moral norms as the necessary and highly valuable guarantee for responsible personal growth in human sexuality".[70] No one is capable of giving moral education in this delicate area better than duly prepared parents.

The Meaning of the Parents' Duty

44. This right also implies *an educational duty.* If in fact parents do not give adequate formation in chastity, they are failing in their precise duty. Likewise, they would also be guilty were they to tolerate immoral or inadequate formation being given to their children outside the home.

45. Today this task encounters a particular difficulty with regard to the dissemination of pornography, through the means of social communication, instigated by commercial motives and breaking down adolescent sensitivity. This must call for two forms of concerned action on the part of parents: preventive and critical education with regard to their children, and courageous denunciation to the appropriate authorities. Parents, as individuals or in associations, have the right and duty to promote the good of their children and demand from the authorities laws that prevent and eliminate the exploitation of the sensitivity of children and adolescents.[71]

46. The Holy Father stresses this parental task and outlines guidelines and the objective in this regard: "Faced with a culture that largely reduces human sexuality to the level of something commonplace, since it interprets and lives it in a reductive and

---

[69] *Familiaris Consortio,* 37; see *Charter of the Rights of the Family,* Article 5, c.

[70] *Familiaris Consortio,* 37.

[71] From the viewpoint of children's education another delicate and complex problem which cannot be taken up sufficiently in this document, is that of the transmission of AIDS sexually and through the use of drugs. The local Churches are involved in many activities to help and support persons with AIDS and for its prevention.

Particularly with regard to preventing AIDS the value of a well-ordered sexuality must be promoted based on the family. Moreover, it is necessary to correct the opinion put about by information campaigns based on so-called "safe sex" and spreading protective means (condoms). This position, in itself contrary to morality, also turns out to be fallacious and ends up increasing promiscuity and free sexual activity through a false idea of safety. Objective and scientifically rigorous studies have shown the high percentage of failure of these means.

impoverished way by linking it solely with the body and with selfish pleasure, the educational service of parents must aim firmly at a training in the area of sex that is truly and fully personal: for sexuality is an enrichment of the whole person — body, emotions and soul — and it manifests its inmost meaning in leading the person to the gift of self in love".[72]

47.   We cannot forget, however, that we are dealing with a right and duty to educate which, in the past, Christian parents carried out or exercised little. Perhaps this was because the problem was not as acute as it is today, or because the parents' task was in part fulfilled by the strength of prevailing social models and the role played by the Church and the Catholic school in this area. It is not easy for parents to take on this educational commitment because today it appears to be rather complex, and greater than what the family could offer, also because, in most cases, it is not possible to refer to what one's own parents did in this regard.

Therefore, through this document, the Church holds that it is her duty to give parents back confidence in their own capabilities and help them to carry out their task.

---

[72] *Familiaris Consortio*, 37.

V

PATHS OF FORMATION WITHIN THE FAMILY

48.   The family environment is thus *the normal and usual place* for forming children and young people to consolidate and exercise the virtues of charity, temperance, fortitude and chastity. As the domestic church, the family is *the school of the richest humanity.*[73] This is particularly true for the moral and spiritual education on such a delicate matter as chastity. Physical, psychological and spiritual aspects are involved in chastity, as well as the first signs of freedom, the influence of social models, natural modesty and strong tendencies inherent in a human being's bodily nature. All of these aspects are connected to an awareness, albeit implicit, of the dignity of the human person, called to collaborate with God and, at the same time, marked by fragility. In a Christian home, parents have the strength to lead their children to a real Christian maturation of their personalities, according to the measure of Christ, in his Mystical Body, the Church.[74]

While the family is rich in these strengths, it also needs the support of the State and society, according to the principle of subsidiarity: "It can happen...that when a family does decide to live up fully to its vocation, it finds itself without the necessary support from the State and without sufficient resources. It is urgent therefore to promote not only family policies, but also those social policies which have the family as their principle object, policies which assist the family by providing adequate resources and efficient means of support, both for bringing up children and for looking after the elderly...".[75]

49.   Aware of this and of the real difficulties that exist for young people in many countries today, especially when social and moral deterioration is present, parents are urged *to dare to ask for more and to propose more.* They cannot be satisfied with avoiding the worst — that their children do not take drugs or commit crimes. They will have to be committed to educating them in the true values of the person, renewed by the virtues of faith, hope and love: the values of freedom, responsibility, fatherhood and motherhood, service, professional work, solidarity, honesty, art, sport, the joy of knowing they are children of God, hence brothers and sisters of all human beings, etc.

---

[73] Cf. *Gaudium et Spes,* 52.
[74] Cf. *Familiaris Consortio,* 39, 51-54.
[75] John Paul II, Encyclical Letter *Centesimus Annus,* May 1, 1991, 49; *AAS* 83 (1991), p. 855.

The Essential Value of the Home

50. In their most recent findings, the psychological and pedagogical sciences come together with human experience in emphasizing the decisive importance of the *affective atmosphere that reigns in the family* for a harmonious and valid sexual education, especially during the first years of infancy and childhood, and perhaps also during the prenatal stage, because children's deep emotional patterns are established in these phases. The importance of the couple's balance, acceptance and understanding is stressed. Furthermore, emphasis is placed on the value of a serene relationship between husband and wife, on the value of their positive presence (both father and mother) during these important years for the processes of identification, and on the value of a relationship of reassuring affection toward their children.

51. Certain serious privations or imbalances between parents (for example, one or both parents' absence from family life, a lack of interest in the children's education or excessive severity) are factors that can cause emotional and affective disturbances in children. These factors can seriously upset their adolescence and sometimes mark them for life. Parents must *find time to be with their children and take time to talk with them.* As a gift and a commitment, children are their most important task, although seemingly not always a very profitable one. Children are more important than work, entertainment and social position. In these conversations — more and more as the years pass — parents should learn how to listen carefully to their children, how to make the effort to understand them, and how to recognize the fragment of truth that may be present in some forms of rebellion. At the same time, parents will have to be able to help their children to channel their anxieties and aspirations correctly, and teach them to reflect on the reality of things and how to reason. This does not mean imposing a certain line of behaviour, but rather showing both the supernatural and human motives that recommend such behaviour. Parents will succeed better if they are able to dedicate time to their children and really place themselves at their level with love.

Formation in the Community of Life and Love

52. The Christian family is capable of offering an atmosphere permeated with that love for God that makes an authentic reciprocal gift possible.[76] Children who have this experience are better disposed to live according to those moral truths that they see practiced in their parents' life. They will have confidence in them and will learn about the love that overcomes fears — and nothing moves us to love more than

---

[76] Cf. *Familiaris Consortio*, 18, 63-64.

knowing that we are loved. In this way, the bond of mutual love, to which parents bear witness before their children, will safeguard their affective serenity. This bond will refine the intellect, the will and the emotions by rejecting everything that could degrade or devalue the gift of human sexuality. In a family where love reigns, this gift *is always understood as part of the call to self-giving in love for God and for others.* "The family is the first and fundamental school of social living: as a community of love, it finds in self-giving the law that guides it and makes it grow. The self-giving that inspires the love of husband and wife for each other is the model and norm for the self-giving that must be practised in the relationships between brothers and sisters and the different generations living together in the family. And the communion and sharing that are part of everyday life in the home at times of joy and at times of difficulty are the most concrete and effective pedagogy for the active, responsible and fruitful inclusion of the children in the wider horizon of society".[77]

53.   Basically, education for authentic love, authentic only if it becomes kind, well-disposed love, involves accepting the person who is loved and considering his or her good as one's own; hence this implies educating in right relationships with others. Children, adolescents and young people should be taught how to enter into healthy relationships with God, with their parents, their brothers and sisters, with their companions of the same or the opposite sex, and with adults.

54.   It must also not be forgotten that *education in love is an overall reality.* There will be no progress in setting up proper relationships with one person if at the same time there are no proper relationships with other people. As we have already mentioned, education in chastity, as education in love, is at the same time education of one's spirit, one's sensitivity, and one's feelings. The attitude toward other persons depends largely on the way spontaneous feelings for them are handled, the way some feelings are cultivated and others are controlled. Chastity as a virtue is never reduced to merely being able to perform acts conforming to a norm of external behaviour. Chastity requires activating and developing the dynamisms of nature and grace which make up the principal and immanent element of our discovery of God's law as a guarantee of growth and freedom.[78]

55.   Therefore, it must be stressed that education for chastity is inseparable from efforts to cultivate *all the other virtues* and, in a particular way, *Christian love,* characterized by respect, altruism and service, which after all is called *charity.* Sexuality is such an important good that it must be protected by following the order of reason

---

[77] *Familiaris Consortio,* 37.
[78] Cf. St. Thomas Aquinas, *Summa Theologiae,* I-II, q. 106, a. 1.

enlightened by faith: "The greater a good, the more the order of reason must be observed in it".[79] From this it follows that in order to educate in chastity, "self-control is necessary, which presupposes such virtues as modesty, temperance, respect for self and for others, openness to one's neighbour".[80]

Also of importance are what Christian tradition has called the younger sisters of chastity (modesty, an attitude of sacrifice with regard to one's whims), nourished by the faith and a life of prayer.

Decency and Modesty

56. *The practice of decency and modesty* in speech, action and dress is very important for creating an atmosphere suitable to the growth of chastity, but this must be well motivated by respect for one's own body and the dignity of others. Parents, as we have said, should be watchful so that certain immoral fashions and attitudes do not violate the integrity of the home, especially through misuse of the *mass media*.[81] In this regard, the Holy Father stressed the need "to promote *closer collaboration* between parents, who have primary responsibility for education, those in charge of the mass media at various levels and the public authorities, so that families are not left without guidance in such an important sector of their educational mission... In fact the presentations, content and programmes of healthy entertainment, information and education to complement that of the family and the school must be recognized. Unfortunately this does not change the fact that in some countries especially there are many shows and publications abounding in all sorts of violence with a kind of bombardment of messages that undermine moral principles and make it impossible to achieve a serious climate in which values worthy of the human person may be transmitted".[82]

In particular, with regard to use of television, the Holy Father specified: "The life-style — especially in the more industrialised nations — all too often causes families to abandon their responsibility to educate their children. Evasion of this duty is made easy by the presence of television and of printed materials in the home. These occupy the time for children and young people. No one can deny the justification for this when the means are lacking, to develop and use to advantage the free time of the young and to direct their energies".[83] Another circumstance that facilitates this is the

---

[79] *Ibid.*, II-II, q. 153, a. 3.

[80] *Educational Guidance in Human Love,* 35.

[81] Cf. *Familiaris Consortio,* 76; cf. also *Educational Guidance in Human Love,* 68; cf. Pontifical Council for Social Communications, *Pornography and Violence in the Communications Media: a Pastoral Response,* May 7, 1989; *L'Osservatore Romano,* English edition, June 5, 1989, pp. 10-11.

[82] John Paul II, *Address* to the participants in a meeting organised by the Pontifical Council for the Family and the Pontifical Council for Social Communications on "The Rights of the Family and the Means of Social Communication", June 4, 1993, 3 and 4; *L'Osservatore Romano,* English edition, July 14, 1993, p. 10.

[83] John Paul II, Message for the Fifteenth Communications Day, May 10, 1981, 5; *L'Osservatore Romano,* English edition, May 29, 1981, p. 7.

fact that both parents are busy with their work, in and outside the home. "The result is that these young people are in most need of help in developing their responsible freedom. There is the duty — especially for believers, for men and women who love freedom, to protect the young from the aggressions they are subjected to by the media. May no one shirk from this duty by using the excuse that he or she is not involved".[84] "Parents as recipients must actively ensure the moderate, critical, watchful and prudent use of the media".[85]

Legitimate Privacy

57. Respect for *privacy* must be considered in close connection with decency and modesty, which spontaneously defend a person who refuses to be considered and treated like an object of pleasure instead of being respected and loved for himself or herself. If children or young people see that their legitimate privacy is respected, then they will know that they are expected to show the same attitude towards others. This is how they learn to cultivate the proper sense of responsibility before God by developing their interior life and a taste for personal freedom, that makes them capable of loving God and others better.

Self-Control

58. All of this reminds us more generally of *self-control,* a necessary condition for being capable of self-giving. Children and young people should be encouraged to have esteem for, and to practise self-control and restraint, to live in an orderly way, to make personal sacrifices in a spirit of love for God, self-respect, and generosity towards others, without stifling feelings and tendencies, but channeling them into a virtuous life.

Parents as Models for Their Children

59. *The good example and leadership of parents* is essential in strengthening the formation of young people in chastity. A mother who values her maternal vocation and her place in the home greatly helps develop the qualities of femininity and motherhood in her daughters, and sets a clear, strong and noble example of womanhood for her sons.[86] A father, whose behaviour is inspired by masculine dignity without

---

[84] *Ibid..*
[85] *Familiaris Consortio,* 76.
[86] Cf. *Mulieris Dignitatem,* 18-19.

"machismo", will be an attractive model for his sons, and inspire respect, admiration and security in his daughters.[87]

60.   This is also true for education in a spirit of sacrifice in families, subject more than ever today to the pressures of materialism and consumerism. Only in this way will children grow up "with a correct attitude of freedom with regard to material goods, by adopting a simple and austere life style and being fully convinced that 'man is more precious for what he is than for what he has'. In a society shaken and split by tensions and conflicts caused by the violent clash of various kinds of individualism and selfishness, children must be enriched not only with a sense of true justice, which alone leads to respect for the personal dignity of each individual, but also and more powerfully by a sense of true love, understood as sincere solicitude and disinterested service with regard to others, especially the poorest and those in most need".[88] "This *education is fully a part of the 'civilization of love'*. It depends on the civilization of love and, in great measure, contributes to its upbuilding".[89]

A Sanctuary of Life and Faith

61.   No one can deny that the first example and the greatest help that parents can give their children is their generosity *in accepting life,* without forgetting that this is how parents help their children to have a simpler lifestyle. Moreover, "...it is certainly less serious to deny their children certain comforts or material advantages than to deprive them of the presence of brothers and sisters, who could help them to grow in humanity and to realize the beauty of life at all its ages and in all its variety".[90]

62.   Lastly, we recall that in order to achieve these objectives, the family first of all should be a *home of faith and prayer,* in which God the Father's presence is sensed, the Word of Jesus is accepted, the Spirit's bond of love is felt, and where the most pure Mother of God is loved and invoked.[91] This life of faith and "Family prayer has for its very own object *family life itself,* which in all its varying circumstances is seen as a call from God and lived as a filial response to his call. Joys and sorrows, hopes and disappointments, births and birthday celebrations, wedding anniversaries of the

---

[87] Cf. *Familiaris Consortio,* 25.

[88] *Ibid.,* 37; cf. also 47-48.

[89] Letter to Families, *Gratissimam Sane,* 16.

[90] John Paul II, *Homily* at Capitol Hall, Washington, D.C., U.S.A., October 7, 1979, 5; *L'Osservatore Romano,* English edition, November 5, 1979, p. 7.

[91] Cf. *Familiaris Consortio,* 59-61; Congregation for the Doctrine of the Faith, Declaration on Certain Questions Concerning Sexual Ethics, *Persona Humana,* December 29, 1975, 11-12; *L'Osservatore Romano,* English edition, January 22, 1976, p. 5.

parents, departures, separations and home-comings, important and far-reaching decisions, the death of those who are dear, etc. — all of these mark God's loving intervention in the family's history. They should be seen as suitable moments for thanksgiving, for petition, for trusting abandonment of the family into the hands of their common Father in heaven".[92]

63.   In this atmosphere of prayer and awareness of the presence and fatherhood of God, the truths of faith and morals should be taught, understood and deeply studied with reverence, and the Word of God should be read and lived with love. In this way Christ's truth will build up a family community based on the example and guidance of parents who "penetrate the innermost depths of their children's hearts and leave an impression that the future events in their lives will not be able to efface".[93]

[92] *Familiaris Consortio,* 59.
[93] *Ibid.,* 60.

VI

LEARNING STAGES

64.   Parents in particular have the duty to let their children know about the *mysteries of human life,* because the family "is, in fact, the best environment to accomplish the obligation of securing a gradual education in sexual life. The family has an affective dignity which is suited to making acceptable without trauma the most delicate realities and to integrating them harmoniously in a balanced and rich personality".[94] As we have recalled, this primary task of the family includes the parents' right that their children should not be obliged to attend courses in school on this subject which are not in harmony with their religious and moral convictions.[95] The school's task is not to substitute for the family, rather it is "assisting and completing the work of parents, furnishing children and adolescents with an evaluation of sexuality as value and task of the whole person, created male and female in the image of God".[96]

In this regard, we recall what the Holy Father teaches in *Familiaris Consortio:* "The Church is firmly opposed to an often widespread form of imparting sex information dissociated from moral principles. That would merely be an introduction to the experience of pleasure and a stimulus leading to the loss of serenity — while still in the years of innocence — by opening the way to vice".[97]

Therefore, *four general principles* will be proposed and afterwards the various stages in a child's development will be examined.

Four Principles Regarding Information about Sexuality

65.   **1. Each child is a unique and unrepeatable person and must receive individualized formation.** Since parents know, understand and love each of their children in their uniqueness, they are in the best position to decide what the appropriate time is for providing a variety of information, according to their children's physical and spiritual growth. No one can take this capacity for discernment away from conscientious parents.[98]

---

[94] *Educational Guidance in Human Love,* 48.
[95] Cf. *Charter of the Rights of the Family,* Article 5, c.
[96] *Educational Guidance in Human Love,* 69.
[97] *Familiaris Consortio,* 37.
[98] Cf. *Ibid.,* 37.

66.   Each child's process of maturation as a person is different. Therefore, the most intimate aspects, whether biological or emotional, should be communicated in *a personalized dialogue*.[99] In their dialogue with each child, with love and trust, parents communicate something about their own self-giving which makes them capable of giving witness to aspects of the emotional dimension of sexuality that could not be transmitted in other ways.

67.   Experience shows that this dialogue works out better when the parent who communicates the biological, emotional, moral and spiritual information is of the same sex as the child or young person. Being aware of the role, emotions and problems of their own sex, mothers have a special bond with their daughters, and fathers with their sons. This natural bond should be respected. Therefore, parents who are alone will have to act with great sensitivity when speaking with a child of the opposite sex, and they may choose to entrust communicating the most intimate details to a trustworthy person of the same sex as the child. Through this collaboration of a subsidiary nature, parents can take advantage of expert, well-formed educators in the school or parish community, or from Catholic associations.

68.   **2. The moral dimension must always be part of their explanations.** Parents should stress that Christians are called to live the gift of sexuality according to the plan of God who is Love, i.e., in the context of marriage or of consecrated virginity and also celibacy.[100] They must insist on the positive value of chastity and its capacity to generate true love for other persons. This is the most radical and important moral aspect of chastity. Only a person who knows how to be chaste will know how to love in marriage or in virginity.

69.   From the earliest age, parents may observe the beginning of instinctive genital activity in their child. It should not be considered repressive to correct such habits gently that could become sinful later, and, when necessary, to teach modesty as the child grows. It is always important to justify the judgement of morally rejecting certain attitudes contrary to the dignity of the person and chastity on adequate, valid and convincing grounds, both at the level of reason and faith, hence in a positive framework with a high concept of personal dignity. Many parental admonitions are merely reproofs or recommendations which the children perceive more as the result of fear of certain social consequences, or related to one's public reputation, rather than arising out of a love that seeks their true good. "I exhort you to correct, with the greatest commitment, the vices and passions that assail us in every age. For if in

---

[99] Cf. *Educational Guidance in Human Love,* 58.
[100] Cf. *Familiaris Consortio,* 16.

some stage of our life we sail on, deprecating the values of virtue and thereby suffer continuous shipwreck, we risk arriving in port devoid of all spiritual charge".[101]

70.   **3. Formation in chastity and timely information regarding sexuality must be provided in the broadest context of education for love.** It is not sufficient, therefore, to provide information about sex together with objective moral principles. Constant help is also required for the growth of children's *spiritual life,* so that the biological development and impulses they begin to experience will always be accompanied by a growing love of God, the Creator and Redeemer, and an ever greater awareness of the dignity of each human person and his or her body. In the light of the mystery of Christ and the Church, parents can illustrate the positive values of human sexuality in the context of the person's original vocation to love and the universal call to holiness.

71.   Therefore, in talks with children, suitable advice should always be given regarding how to grow in the love of God and one's neighbour; and how to overcome any difficulties: "These means are: discipline of the senses and the mind, watchfulness and prudence in avoiding occasions of sin, the observance of modesty, moderation in recreation, wholesome pursuits, assiduous prayer and frequent reception of the Sacraments of Penance and the Eucharist. Young people especially should foster devotion to the Immaculate Mother of God".[102]

72.   To teach children how to evaluate the environments they frequent with a critical sense and true autonomy, as well as to accustom them to detachment in using the mass media, parents should always present positive models and suitable ways of using their vital energies, the meaning of friendship and solidarity in the overall area of society and of the Church.

When deviant tendencies and attitudes are present, which require great prudence and caution so as to recognize and evaluate situations properly, parents should also have recourse to specialists with solid scientific and moral formation in order to identify the causes over and above the symptoms, and help the subjects to overcome difficulties in a serious and clear way. Pedagogic action should be directed more to the causes rather than to directly repressing the phenomenon,[103] and, if necessary, they should seek the help of qualified persons, such as doctors, educational experts and psychologists with an upright Christian sensitivity.

73.   The objective of the parents' educational task is to pass on to their children the conviction *that chastity in one's state in life is possible and that chastity brings joy.* Joy

---

[101] St. John Chrysostom, *Homiliae in Matthaeum,* 81, 5: PG 58, 737.

[102] *Persona Humana,* 12.

[103] Cf. *Ibid.,* 9; *Educational Guidance in Human Love,* 99.

springs from an awareness of maturation and harmony in one's emotional life, a gift of God and a gift of love that makes self-giving possible in the framework of one's vocation. Man is in fact the only creature on earth whom God wanted for its own sake, and "man can fully discover his true self only in a sincere giving of himself".[104] "Christ gave laws for everyone...I do not prohibit you from marrying, nor am I against your enjoying yourself. I only want you to do this with temperance, without indecency, guilt and sin. I do not make a law that you should flee to the mountains and deserts, rather that you should be good, modest and chaste, as you live in the midst of the cities".[105]

74.   God's help is never lacking if each person makes the necessary commitment to respond to his grace. In helping, forming and respecting their children's conscience, parents should see that they receive *the sacraments* with awareness, guiding them by their own example. If children and young people experience the effects of God's grace and mercy in the sacraments, they will be capable of living chastity well, as a gift of God, for his glory and in order to love him and other people. Necessary and supernaturally effective help is provided by the Sacrament of Reconciliation, especially if a regular confessor is available. Although it does not necessarily coincide with the role of confessor, spiritual guidance or direction is a valuable aid in progressively enlightening the stages of growth and as moral support.

Reading well-chosen and recommended books of formation is also of great help both in offering a wider and deeper formation and in providing examples and testimonies of virtue.

75.   Once the objectives of the information to be provided have been identified, the time and ways must be specified, starting from childhood.

4. Parents should provide this information with great delicacy, but clearly and at the appropriate time. Parents are well aware that their children must be treated in a personalized way, according to the personal conditions of their physiological and psychological development, and taking into due consideration the cultural environment of life and the adolescent's daily experience. In order to evaluate properly what they should say to each child, it is very important that parents first of all seek light from the Lord in prayer and that they discuss this together so that their words will be neither too explicit nor too vague. Giving too many details to children is counterproductive. But delaying the first information for too long is imprudent, because every human person has natural curiosity in this regard and, sooner or later, everyone begins to ask themselves questions, especially in cultures where too much can be seen, even in public.

---

[104] *Gaudium et Spes,* 24.
[105] St. John Chrysostom, *Homiliae in Matthaeum,* 7,7: PG 57, 80-81.

76.   In general, the first sexual information to be given to a small child does not deal with genital sexuality, but rather with pregnancy and the birth of a brother or sister. The child's natural curiosity is stimulated, for example, when it sees the signs of pregnancy in its mother and experiences waiting for a baby. Parents can take advantage of this happy experience in order to communicate some simple facts about pregnancy, but always in the deepest context of wonder at the creative work of God, who wants the new life he has given to be cared for in the mother's body, near her heart.

Children's Principal Stages of Development

77.   It is important for parents to take their children's needs into consideration during the different stages of development. Keeping in mind that each child should receive individualized formation, parents can adapt the stages of education in love to the particular requirements of each child.

1. The Years of Innocence

78.   It can be said that a child is in the stage described in John Paul II's words as *"the years of innocence"* [106] from about five years of age until puberty — the beginning of which can be set at the first signs of changes in the boy or girl's body (the visible effect of an increased production of sexual hormones). This period of tranquility and serenity must never be disturbed by unnecessary information about sex. During those years, before any physical sexual development is evident, it is normal for the child's interests to turn to other aspects of life. The rudimentary instinctive sexuality of very small children has disappeared. Boys and girls of this age are not particularly interested in sexual problems, and they prefer to associate with children of their own sex. So as not to disturb this important natural phase of growth, parents will recognize that prudent formation in chaste love during this period should be indirect, in preparation for puberty, when direct information will be necessary.

79.   During this stage of development, children are normally at ease with their body and its functions. They accept the need for modesty in dress and behaviour. Although they are aware of the physical differences between the two sexes, the growing child generally shows little interest in genital functions. The discovery of the wonders of creation which accompanies this phase and the experiences in this regard at home and in school should also be oriented towards the stages of catechesis and preparation for the sacraments which takes place within the ecclesial community.

[106] *Familiaris Consortio, 37.*

80. Nonetheless, this period of childhood is not without its own significance in terms of psycho-sexual development. A growing boy or girl is learning from adult example and family experience *what it means to be a woman or a man.* Certainly, expressions of natural tenderness and sensitivity should not be discouraged among boys, nor should girls be excluded from vigorous physical activities. On the other hand, in some societies subjected to ideological pressures, parents should also protect themselves from an exaggerated opposition to what is defined as a "stereotyping of roles". The real differences between the two sexes should not be ignored or minimized, and in a healthy family environment children will learn that it is natural for a certain difference to exist between the usual family and domestic roles of men and women.

81. During this stage, girls will generally be developing a maternal interest in babies, motherhood and homemaking. By constantly taking the Motherhood of the most holy Virgin Mary as a model, they should be encouraged to value their femininity.

82. In this period, a boy is at a relatively tranquil stage of development. This is often the easiest time for him to set up a good relationship with his father. At this time, he should learn that, although it must be considered as a divine gift, his masculinity is not a sign of superiority with regard to women, but a call from God to take on certain roles and responsibilities. Boys should be discouraged from becoming overly aggressive or too concerned about physical prowess as proof of their virility.

83. Nonetheless, in the context of moral and sexual information, various problems can arise in this stage of childhood. In some societies today, there are planned and determined attempts to impose *premature sex information* on children. But, at this stage of development, children are still not capable of fully understanding the value of the affective dimension of sexuality. They cannot understand and control sexual imagery within the proper context of moral principles and, for this reason, they cannot integrate premature sexual information with moral responsibility. Such information tends to shatter their emotional and educational development and to disturb the natural serenity of this period of life. Parents should politely but firmly exclude any attempts to violate children's innocence because such attempts compromise the spiritual, moral and emotional development of growing persons who have a right to their innocence.

84. A further problem arises when children receive premature sex information from the mass media or from their peers who have been led astray or received premature sex education. In this case, parents will have to begin to give carefully limited

sexual information, usually to correct immoral and erroneous information or to control obscene language.

85.   Sexual violence with regard to children is not infrequent. Parents must protect their children, first by teaching them a form of modesty and reserve with regard to strangers, as well as by giving suitable sexual information, but without going into details and particulars that might upset or frighten them.

86.   As in the first years of life also during childhood, parents should encourage a spirit of collaboration, obedience, generosity and self-denial in their children, as well as a capacity for self-reflection and sublimation. In fact, a characteristic of this period of development is an attraction toward intellectual activities. Using the intellect makes it possible to acquire the strength and ability to control the surrounding situation and, before long, to control bodily instincts, so as to transform them into intellectual and rational activities.

An undisciplined or spoilt child is inclined toward a certain immaturity and moral weakness in future years because chastity is difficult to maintain if a person develops selfish or disordered habits and cannot behave with proper concern and respect for others. Parents should present objective standards of what is right and wrong, thereby creating a sure moral framework for life.

2. Puberty

87.   Puberty, which constitutes the initial phase of adolescence, is a time in which parents are called to be particularly attentive to the *Christian education of their children*. This is a time of self-discovery and "of one's own inner world, the time of generous plans, the time when the feeling of love awakens, with the biological impulses of sexuality, the time of the desire to be together, the time of particularly intense joy connected with the exhilarating discovery of life. But often it is also the age of deeper questioning, of anguished or even frustrating searching, of a certain mistrust of others and dangerous introspection, and the age sometimes of the first experiences of setbacks and of disappointments".[107]

88.   Parents should pay particular attention to their children's gradual development and to their physical and psychological changes, which are decisive in the maturing of the personality. Without showing anxiety, fear or obsessive concern, parents will not let cowardice or convenience hinder their work. This is naturally an important moment for teaching the value of chastity, which will also be expressed in the way

---

[107] John Paul II, Apostolic Exhortation *Catechesi Tradendae,* October 16, 1979, 38; *AAS* 71 (1979), p. 1309.

sexual information is given. In this phase, educational needs also concern the genital aspects, hence requiring a presentation both on the level of values and the reality as a whole. Moreover, this implies an understanding of the context of procreation, marriage and the family, a context which must be kept present in an authentic task of sexual education.[108]

89.   Beginning with the changes which their sons and daughters experience in their bodies, parents are thus bound to give *more detailed explanations about sexuality* (in an on-going relationship of trust and friendship) each time girls confide in their mothers and boys in their fathers. This relationship of trust and friendship should have already started in the first years of life.

90.   Another important task for parents is following the gradual physiological development of their daughters and helping them joyfully to accept *the development of their femininity* in a bodily, psychological and spiritual sense.[109] Therefore, normally, one should discuss the cycles of fertility and their meaning. But it is still not necessary to give detailed explanations about sexual union, unless this is explicitly requested.

91.   It is very important for adolescent boys to be helped to understand the stages of physical and physiological development of the genital organs before they get this information from their companions or from persons who are not well-intentioned. The physiological facts about male puberty should be presented in an atmosphere of serenity, positively and with reserve, in the framework of marriage, family and fatherhood. Instructing both adolescent girls and boys should also include detailed and sufficient information about the bodily and psychological characteristics of the opposite sex, about whom their curiosity is growing.

In this area, the additional supportive information of a conscientious doctor or even a psychologist can help parents, without separating this information from what pertains to the faith and the educational work of the priest.

92.   Through *a trusting and open dialogue,* parents can guide *their daughters* in facing any emotional perplexity, and support the value of Christian chastity out of consideration for the other sex. Instruction for both girls and boys should aim at pointing out the beauty of motherhood and the wonderful reality of procreation, as well as the deep meaning of virginity. In this way they will be helped to go against the hedonistic mentality which is very widespread today and particularly, at such a decisive stage,

---

[108] This positive attitude is deeply rooted in many cultures and puberty is celebrated with "rites of passage" or forms of initiation into adult life. Under the careful guidance of the Church, Catholics can take on what is good and authentic in these customs, purifying them from what may be inadequate or immoral.

[109] Cf. *Mulieris Dignitatem,* 17 ff.

in preventing the *"contraceptive mentality"*, which unfortunately is very common and which girls will have to face later in marriage.

93.   During puberty, *the psychological and emotional development of boys* can make them vulnerable to erotic fantasies and they may be tempted to try sexual experiences. Parents should be close to their sons and correct the tendency to use sexuality in a hedonistic and materialistic way. Therefore, they should remind boys about God's gift, received in order to cooperate with him "to actualize in history the original blessing of the Creator — that of transmitting by procreation the divine image from person to person..."; and this will strengthen their awareness that, "Fecundity is the fruit and the sign of conjugal love, the living testimony of the full reciprocal self-giving of the spouses".[110] In this way sons will also learn the respect due to women. The parents' task of informing and instructing is necessary, not because their sons would not know about sexual reality in other ways, but so that they will know about it in the right light.

94.   In a *positive and prudent* way, parents will carry out what the Fathers of the Second Vatican Council requested: "It is important to give suitable and timely instruction to young people, above all in the heart of their own families, about the dignity of married love, its role and its exercise; in this way they will be able to engage in honourable courtship and enter upon marriage of their own".[111]

Positive information about sexuality should always be part of a formation plan so as to create the Christian context in which all information about life, sexual activity, anatomy and hygiene is given. Therefore, the spiritual and moral dimensions must always be predominant so as to have two special purposes: presenting God's commandments as a way of life, and the formation of a right conscience.

To the young man who asked him what he had to do in order to attain eternal life, Jesus replied: "If you would enter life, keep the commandments" (*Matthew* 19:17). After listing the ones that concern love for one's neighbour, Jesus summed them up in this positive formulation: "You shall love your neighbour as yourself" (*Matthew* 19:19). In order to present the commandments as God's gift (written by his hand, cf. *Exodus* 31: 18), expressing the Covenant with him, confirmed by Jesus' own example, it is very important for the adolescent not to separate the commandments from their relationship with a rich interior life, free from selfishness.[112]

---

[110] *Familiaris Consortio*, 28; cf. also *Gaudium et Spes*, 50.
[111] *Gaudium et Spes*, 49.
[112] Cf. *Catechism of the Catholic Church*, 2052 ff.

95.   As its departure point, the formation of conscience requires being enlightened about: God's project of love for every single person, the positive and liberating value of the moral law, and awareness both of the weakness caused by sin and the means of grace which strengthen us on our path towards the good and towards salvation.

"Moral conscience, present at the heart of the person" — which is "man's most secret core and sanctuary", as the Second Vatican Council affirms,[113] "enjoins him at the appropriate moment to do good and to avoid evil. It also judges particular choices, approving those that are good and denouncing those that are evil. It bears witness to the authority of truth in reference to the supreme Good to which the human person is drawn, and it welcomes the commandments".[114]

In fact, "conscience is a judgement of reason whereby the human person recognizes the moral quality of a concrete act that he is going to perform, is in the process of performing, or has already completed".[115] Therefore, the formation of conscience requires being enlightened about the truth and God's plan and must not be confused with a vague subjective feeling or with personal opinion.

96.   In answering *children's questions,* parents should offer well-reasoned arguments about the great value of chastity and show the intellectual and human weakness of theories that inspire permissive and hedonistic behaviour. They will answer clearly, without giving excessive importance to pathological sexual problems. Nor will they give the false impression that sex is something shameful or dirty, because it is a great gift of God who placed the ability to generate life in the human body, thereby sharing his creative power with us. Indeed, both in the Scriptures (cf. *Song of Songs* 1-8; *Hosea* 2; *Jeremiah* 3: 1-3; *Ezekial* 23, etc.) and in the Christian mystical tradition,[116] conjugal love has always been considered a symbol and image of God's love for us.

97.   Since boys and girls at puberty are particularly vulnerable to *emotional influences,* through dialogue and the way they live, parents have the duty to help their children resist negative outside influences that may lead them to have little regard for Christian formation in love and chastity. Especially in societies overwhelmed by consumer pressures, parents should sometimes watch out for their children's relations with young people of the opposite sex — without making it too obvious. Even if they are socially acceptable, some habits of speech and conduct are not morally correct and represent a way of trivializing sexuality, reducing it to a consumer object. Parents should therefore teach their children the value of Christian modesty, moderate dress, and, when it comes to trends, the necessary autonomy characteristic of a man or woman with a mature personality.[117]

[113] *Gaudium et Spes,* 16.
[114] *Catechism of the Catholic Church,* 1777.
[115] *Ibid.,* 1778.
[116] Cf. St. Teresa of Avila, *Poems,* 5-9; St. John of the Cross, *Poems,* 10.
[117] Cf. *Educational Guidance in Human Love,* 90.

3. Adolescence in One's Plan in Life

98.   In terms of personal development, adolescence represents the period of self-projection and therefore the discovery of one's vocation. Both for physiological, social and cultural reasons, this period tends to be longer today than in the past. Christian parents should "educate the children for life in such a way that each one may fully perform his or her role according to the *vocation received from God*".[118] This is an extremely important task which basically constitutes the culmination of the parents' mission. Although this task is always important, it becomes especially so in this period of their children's life: "Therefore, in the life of each member of the lay faithful there are *particularly significant and decisive moments* for discerning God's call...Among these are the periods of *adolescence* and *young adulthood*".[119]

99.   It is very important for young people not to find themselves alone in discerning their *personal vocation*. Parental advice is relevant, at times decisive, as well as the support of a priest or other properly formed persons (in parishes, associations or in the new fruitful ecclesial movements, etc.) who are capable of helping them discover the vocational meaning of life and the various forms of the universal call to holiness. "Christ's *'Follow me'* makes itself heard on the different paths taken by the disciples and confessors of the divine Redeemer".[120]

100.   For centuries, the concept of vocation was reserved exclusively for the priesthood and religious life. In recalling the Lord's teaching, "You, therefore, must be perfect, as your heavenly Father is perfect" (*Matthew* 5:48), the Second Vatican Council renewed the universal call to holiness.[121] As Pope Paul VI wrote shortly after the Council: "This strong invitation to holiness could be regarded as the most characteristic element in the whole Magisterium of the Council, and so to say, its ultimate purpose".[122] This was reiterated by Pope John Paul II: "The Second Vatican Council has significantly spoken on the universal call to holiness. It is possible to say that this call to holiness is precisely the basic charge entrusted to all the sons and daughters of the Church by a Council which intended to bring a renewal of Christian life based on the gospel.[123] This charge is not a simple moral exhortation, but an *undeniable requirement arising from the mystery of the Church*".[124]

God calls everyone to holiness. He has very precise plans for each person, a *personal vocation* which each must recognize, accept and develop. To all Christians —

---

[118]   *Familiaris Consortio*, 53.

[119]   *Christifideles Laici*, 58.

[120]   John Paul II, Apostolic Letter to the Young People of the World, *Parati Semper*, March 31, 1985; *L'Osservatore Romano*, April 1, 1985, p. 1, 9.

[121]   Cf. *Lumen Gentium*, Chapter V.

[122]   Paul VI, Motu Proprio, *Sanctitatis Clarior*, March 19, 1969; *AAS* 61 (1969), p. 149.

[123]   See, in particular, *Lumen Gentium*, Chapter V, 39-42, which deals with the *universal call to holiness in the Church*.

[124]   *Christifideles Laici*, 16.

priests, laity, married people or celibates — the words of the Apostle of the Nations apply: *"God's chosen ones, holy and beloved"* (*Colossians* 3:12).

101.   Therefore, in catechesis and the formation given both within and outside of the family, the Church's teaching on the sublime value of virginity and celibacy must never be lacking,[125] but also the vocational meaning of marriage, which a Christian can never regard as only a human venture. As St. Paul says "This is a great mystery, and I mean in reference to Christ and the church." (*Ephesians* 5:32). Giving young people this firm conviction is of supreme importance for the good both of the Church and humanity which "depend in great part on parents and on the family life that they build in their homes".[126]

102.   Parents should always strive to give *example and witness* with their own lives to fidelity to God and one another in the marriage covenant. Their example is especially decisive in adolescence, the phase when young people are looking for *lived and attractive behaviour models*. Since sexual problems become more evident at this time, parents should also help them to love the beauty and strength of chastity through prudent advice, highlighting the inestimable value of prayer and frequent fruitful recourse to the sacraments for a chaste life, especially personal confession. Furthermore, parents should be capable of giving their children, when necessary, a positive and serene explanation of the solid points of Christian morality such as, for example, the indissolubility of marriage and the relationship between love and procreation, as well as the immorality of premarital relations, abortion, contraception and masturbation. With regard to these immoral situations that contradict the meaning of giving in marriage, it is also good to recall that: *"The two dimensions of conjugal union,* the unitive and the procreative, *cannot be artificially separated* without damaging the deepest truth of the conjugal act itself".[127] In this regard, an in-depth and reflective knowledge of the documents of the Church dealing with these problems will be of valuable assistance to parents.[128]

---

[125] Cf. Tertullian, *De Exhortatione Castitatis,* 10: CChL 2, 1029-1030; St. Cyprian, *De Habitu Virginum,* 3 and 22: CSEL 3/1, 189, 202-203; St. Athanasius, *De Virginitate:* PG 28, 252-281; St. John Chrysostom, *De Virginitate:* SCh 125; Pius XII, Apostolic Exhortation, *Menti Nostrae,* September 23, 1950; AAS 42 (1950), p. 682; John XXIII, *Address* to the participants in the First International Congress on "The Vocations to States of Perfection in the World Today", organized by the Sacred Congregation for Religious, December 16, 1961; AAS 54 (1962), p. 33; *Lumen Gentium,* 42; *Familiaris Consortio,* 16.

[126] John Paul II, *Homily* at the Mass in Limerick (Ireland), October 1, 1979; *L'Osservatore Romano,* English edition, October 15, 1979, pp. 6-7.

[127] Letter to Families, *Gratissimam Sane,* 12.

[128] In addition to *Gaudium et Spes,* 47-52, *Humanae Vitae* and *Familiaris Consortio,* there are other important Documents at their disposal such as: the Congregation for the Doctrine of the Faith, *Persona Humana* and the *Letter to Bishops of the Catholic Church on The Pastoral Care of Homosexual Persons,* October 1, 1986; *L'Osservatore Romano,* English edition, November 10, 1986, pp. 2-3, and the Congregation for Catholic Education, *Educational Guidance in Human Love,* together with the teaching of the *Catechism of the Catholic Church,* 2331-2400, 2514-2533.

103. *Masturbation* particularly constitutes a very serious disorder that is illicit in itself and cannot be morally justified, although "the immaturity of adolescence (which can sometimes persist after that age), psychological imbalance or habit can influence behaviour, diminishing the deliberate character of the act and bringing about a situation whereby subjectively there may not always be serious fault".[129] Therefore, adolescents should be helped to overcome manifestations of this disorder, which often express the inner conflicts of their age and, in many cases, a selfish vision of sexuality.

104. A particular problem that can appear during the process of sexual maturation is *homosexuality,* which is also spreading more and more in urbanized societies. This phenomenon must be presented with balanced judgement, in the light of the documents of the Church.[130] Young people need to be helped to distinguish between the concepts of what is normal and abnormal, between subjective guilt and objective disorder, avoiding what would arouse hostility. On the other hand, the structural and complementary orientation of sexuality must be well clarified in relation to marriage, procreation and Christian chastity. "Homosexuality refers to relations between men or between women who experience an exclusive or predominant sexual attraction toward persons of the same sex. It has taken a great variety of forms through the centuries and in different cultures. Its psychological genesis remains largely unexplained".[131] A distinction must be made between a tendency that can be innate and acts of homosexuality that "are intrinsically disordered" [132] and contrary to Natural Law.[133]

Especially when the practice of homosexual acts has not become a habit, many cases can benefit from appropriate therapy. In any case, persons in this situation must be accepted with respect, dignity and delicacy, and all forms of unjust discrimination must be avoided. If parents notice the appearance of this tendency or of related behaviour in their children, during childhood or adolescence, they should seek help from expert qualified persons in order to obtain all possible assistance.

For most homosexual persons, this condition constitutes a trial. "They must be accepted with respect, compassion and sensitivity. Every sign of unjust discrimination in their regard should be avoided. These persons are called to fulfil God's will in their lives and, if they are Christians, to unite to the sacrifice of the Lord's Cross the difficulties they may encounter from their condition".[134] "Homosexual persons are called to chastity".[135]

---

[129] *Persona Humana,* 9.
[130] Documents of the Congregation for the Doctrine of the Faith: *Persona Humana* and *The Pastoral Care of Homosexual Persons* as well as the *Catechism of the Catholic Church,* 2357-2359.
[131] *Catechism of the Catholic Church,* 2357.
[132] *Persona Humana,* 8.
[133] Cf. *Catechism of the Catholic Church,* 2357.
[134] *Ibid.,* 2358
[135] *Ibid.,* 2359

105.   Awareness of the positive significance of sexuality for personal harmony and development, as well as the person's vocation in the family, society and the Church, always represents the educational horizon to be presented during the stages of adolescent growth. It must never be forgotten that the disordered use of sex tends progressively to destroy *the person's capacity to love* by making pleasure, instead of sincere self-giving, the end of sexuality and by reducing other persons to objects of one's own gratification. In this way the meaning of true love between a man and a woman (love always open to life) is weakened as well as the family itself. Moreover, this subsequently leads to disdain for the human life which could be conceived, which, in some situations, is then regarded as an evil that threatens personal pleasure.[136] "The trivialization of sexuality is among the principal factors which have led to contempt for new life. Only a true love is able to protect life".[137]

106.   We must also remember how adolescents in industrialized societies are preoccupied and at times disturbed not only by the problems of *self-identity,* discovering their plan in life and difficulties in successfully integrating sexuality in a mature and well-oriented personality. They also have problems in accepting themselves and their bodies. In this regard, out-patient and specialized centres for adolescents have now sprung up, often characterized by purely hedonistic purposes. On the other hand, a healthy culture of the body leads to accepting oneself as a gift and as an incarnated spirit, called to be open to God and society. A healthy culture of the body should accompany formation in this very constructive period, which is also not without its risks.

In the face of what hedonistic groups propose, especially in affluent societies, it is very important to present young people with the ideals of human and Christian solidarity and concrete ways of being committed in Church associations, movements and voluntary Catholic and missionary activities.

107.   *Friendships* are very important in this period. According to local social conditions and customs, adolescence is a time when young people enjoy more autonomy in their relations with others and in the hours they keep in family life. Without taking away their rightful autonomy, when necessary, parents should know how to say "no" to their children[138] and, at the same time, they should know how to cultivate a taste in

---

[136] Together with awareness of the particular strength of the *libido* — revealed by study of the human psyche — this helps us understand the teaching of the Church regarding the seriousness of any disordered use of sex. "According to Christian tradition and as right reason also recognizes, the moral order of sexuality involves such high values of human life that every direct violation of this order is objectively serious.", *Persona humana,* 10. (Note that the Church teaches the serious character because of the object of the act, but this does not exclude the absence of grave guilt owing to the imperfection of the will. Indeed, in the same number of *Persona Humana,* it is made clear that in this area such imperfection in quite possible).

[137] *Evangelium Vitae,* 97

[138] One only has to think of the abuses that often take place in some discotheques, even among boys and girls under 16 years of age.

their children for what is beautiful, noble and true. Parents should also be sensitive to adolescents' self-esteem, which may pass through a confused phase when they are not clear about what personal dignity means and requires.

108.   Through loving and patient advice, parents will help young people to avoid *an excessive closing in on themselves*. When necessary, they will also teach them to go against social trends that tend to stifle true love and an appreciation for spiritual realities: "Be sober, be watchful. Your adversary the devil prowls around like a roaring lion, seeking some one to devour. Resist him, firm in your faith, knowing that the same experience of suffering is required of your brotherhood throughout the world. And after you have suffered a little while, the God of all grace, who has called you to his eternal glory in Christ, will himself restore, establish, and strengthen you" (*1 Peter* 5:8-10).

4. Towards Adulthood

109.   It is not within the scope of this document to deal with the subject of proximate and immediate preparation for marriage, required for Christian formation and particularly recommended by the needs of the times and Church teaching.[139] Nevertheless, it must be kept in mind that the parents' mission does not end when their children come of legal age which, in any case, varies according to different cultures and laws. Some particularly significant moments for young people are also when they enter the working world or higher education, moments when they come into contact with different behaviour models and occasions that represent a real personal challenge — a brusque contact at times, but a potentially beneficial one.

110.   By keeping open a confident dialogue that encourages a sense of responsibility and respects their children's legitimate and necessary autonomy, parents will always be their reference point, through both advice and example, so that the process of broader socialization will make it possible for them to achieve a mature and integrated personality, internally and socially. In a special way, care should be taken that children do not discontinue their faith relationship with the Church and her activities which, on the contrary, should be intensified. They should learn how to choose models of thought and life for their future and how to become committed in the cultural and social area as Christians, without fear of professing that they are Christians and without losing a sense of vocation and the search for their own vocation.

In the period leading to *engagement* and the choice of that prefered attachment which can lead to forming a family, the role of parents should not consist merely in

[139] Cf. *Familiaris Consortio*, 66.

prohibitions, much less in imposing the choice of a fiancé or fiancée. On the contrary, they should help their children to define the necessary conditions for a serious, honorable and promising union, and support them on a path of clear and coherent Christian witness in relating with the person of the other sex.

111. Parents should avoid adopting the widespread mentality whereby girls are given every recommendation regarding virtue and the value of virginity, while the same is not required for boys, as if everything were licit for them.

For a Christian conscience and a vision of marriage and the family, St. Paul's recommendation to the Philippians holds for every type of vocation: "...whatever is true, whatever is honourable, whatever is just, whatever is pure, whatever is lovely, whatever is gracious, if there is any excellency, if there is anything worthy of praise, think about these things" (*Philippians* 4:8).

VII

PRACTICAL GUIDELINES

112.   In the context of education in the virtues, parents thus have the task of making themselves the promoters of their children's authentic education for love. Through its very nature, the *primary* generation of a human life in the procreative act must be followed by the secondary generation, whereby parents help their child to develop his or her own personality.

Therefore, summing up what has been said so far and putting it on a practical level, whatever is set out in the following paragraphs is *recommended*.[140]

Recommendations for Parents and Educators

113.   *It is recommended that parents be aware of their own educational role and defend and carry out this primary right and duty*.[141] It follows that any educative activity, related to education for love and carried out by persons outside the family, must be subject to the parents' acceptance of it and must be seen not as a substitute but as a support for their work. In fact, "Sex education, which is a basic right and duty of parents, must always be carried out under their attentive guidance whether at home or in educational centres chosen and controlled by them".[142] Frequently parents are not lacking in awareness and effort, but they are quite alone, defenceless and often made to feel they are wrong. They need understanding, but also support and help by groups, associations and institutions.

1. *Recommendations for Parents*

114. 1. It is recommended that *parents associate with other parents,* not only in order to protect, maintain or fill out their own role as the primary educators of their chil-

---

[140] The following recommendations have been formulated: (a) in the light of the right of every person to believe and practise the Catholic Faith: cf. Second Vatican Council, Declaration on Religious Freedom, *Dignitatis Humanae,* 1, 2, 5, 13, 14; *Charter of the Rights of the Family,* Article 7; (b) in terms of the rights, freedom and dignity of the family: cf. Preamble of the *Charter of the Rights of the Family; Dignitatis Humanae,* 5; *Familiaris Consortio,* 26, 42, 46.

[141] Cf. *Gravissimum Educationis,* 3; *Familiaris Consortio,* 36; *Charter of the Rights of the Family,* Article 5.

[142] *Familiaris Consortio,* 37.

dren, especially in the area of education for love,[143] but also to fight against damaging forms of sex education and to ensure that their children will be educated according to Christian principles and in a way that is consonant with their personal development.

115. 2. In the case where parents are helped by others in educating their own children for love, it is recommended that *they keep themselves precisely informed on the content and methodology with which such supplementary education is imparted.*[144] No one can bind children or young people to secrecy about the content and method of instruction provided outside the family.

116. 3. We are aware of the difficulty and often the impossibility for parents *to participate fully in all supplementary instruction provided outside the home.* Nevertheless, they have the right to be informed about the structure and content of the programme. In all cases, their right to be present during classes cannot be denied.[145]

117. 4. It is recommended that parents attentively follow every form of sex education that is given to their children outside the home, *removing their children whenever this education does not correspond to their own principles.*[146] However, such a decision of the parents must not become grounds for discrimination against their children.[147] On the other hand, parents who remove their children from such instruction have the duty to give them an adequate formation, appropriate to each child or young person's stage of development.

2. Recommendations for All Educators

118. 1. Since each child or young person must be able to live his or her own sexuality in conformity with Christian principles, and hence be able to exercise the virtue of chastity, *no educator — not even parents — can interfere with this right to chastity* (cf. *Matthew* 18: 4-7).[148]

---

[143] Cf. *Charter of the Rights of the Family*, Articles 8 a. and 5 c. *Code of Canon Law*, January 25, 1983, Canons 215, 223 § 2, 799; Letter to Families, *Gratissimam Sane*, 16.

[144] This recommendation is derived from the *Charter of the Rights of the Family*, Article 5 c., d., e., because the right to know implies supervision and control on the part of parents.

[145] This recommendation is derived from the *Charter of the Rights of the Family*, Article 5 c., d., e., because parents' participation facilitates the supervision and control of their children's education for love.

[146] This recommendation in derived from the *Charter of the Rights of the Family*, Article 5 c., d., e., because the right to remove children from sexual formation gives parents the freedom to exercise their right to educate their children according to their conscience (Article 5 a. of the *Charter*).

[147] Cf. *Charter of the Rights of the Family*, Article 7.

[148] *Ibid.*, Article 4 e.

119. 2. It is recommended that respect be given to *the right of the child and the young person to be adequately informed* by their own parents on moral and sexual questions in a way that complies with his or her desire to be chaste and to be formed in chastity.[149] This right is further qualified by a child's stage of development, his or her capacity to integrate moral truth with sexual information, and by respect for his or her innocence and tranquility.

120. 3. It is recommended that respect be given to *the right of the child or young person to withdraw from any form of sexual instruction imparted outside the home*.[150] Neither the children nor other members of their family should ever be penalized or discriminated against for this decision.

Four Working Principles and Their Particular Norms

121. In the light of these recommendations, education for love can take concrete form in four *working principles*.

122. 1. **Human sexuality is a sacred mystery and must be presented according to the doctrinal and moral teaching of the Church, always bearing in mind the effects of original sin.**
Informed by Christian reverence and realism, this *doctrinal principle* must guide every moment of education for love. In an age when the mystery has been taken from human sexuality, parents must take care to avoid trivializing human sexuality, in their teaching and in the help offered by others. In particular, profound respect must be maintained for the difference between man and woman which reflects the love and fruitfulness of God himself.

123. At the same time, when teaching Catholic doctrine and morality about sexuality, *the lasting effects of original sin* must be taken into account, that is to say, human weakness and the need for the grace of God to overcome temptations and avoid sin. In this regard, the *conscience* of every individual must be *formed* clearly, precisely and in accord with spiritual values. But Catholic morality is never limited to teaching about avoiding sin. It also deals with growth in the Christian virtues and developing the capacity for self-giving in the vocation of one's own life.

124. 2. **Only information proportionate to each phase of their individual development should be presented to children and young people.**

---

[149] This recommendation is derived from *Gravissimum Educationis,* 1.
[150] This recommendation is the practical extension of the right of the child to be chaste, n. 118 above, and corresponds to the parents' right, n. 117 above.

This principle of timing has already been presented in the study of the various phases of the development of children and young people. Parents and all who help them should be sensitive: (*a*) to the different phases of development, in particular, the "years of innocence" and puberty, (*b*) to the way each child or young person experiences the various stages of life, (*c*) to particular problems associated with these stages.

125. In the light of this principle, the relevance of timing in relation to specific problems can also be indicated.

(*a*) In later adolescence, young people can first be introduced to the knowledge of the signs of fertility and then to the *natural regulation of fertility*, but only in the context of education for love, fidelity in marriage, God's plan for procreation and respect for human life.

(*b*) *Homosexuality* should not be discussed before adolescence unless a specific serious problem has arisen in a particular situation.[151] This subject must be presented only in terms of chastity, health and "the truth about human sexuality in its relationship to the family as taught by the Church".[152]

(*c*) *Sexual perversions* that are relatively rare should not be dealt with except through individual counselling, as the parents' response to genuine problems.

126. 3. **No material of an erotic nature should be presented to children or young people of any age, individually or in a group.**

This *principle of decency* must safeguard the virtue of Christian chastity.

Therefore, in passing on sexual information in the context of education for love, the instruction must always be *"positive and prudent"* [153] and *"clear and delicate"*.[154] These four words used by the Catholic Church exclude every form of *unacceptable content in sexual education*.[155]

Moreover, even if they are not erotic, graphic and realistic representations of childbirth, for example in a film, should be made known gradually, so as not to create fear and negative attitudes towards procreation in girls and young women.

127. 4. **No one should ever be invited, let alone obliged, to act in any way that could objectively offend against modesty or which could subjectively offend against his or her own delicacy or sense of privacy.**

---

[151] Cf. *Educational Guidance in Human Love*, 101-103.

[152] *The Pastoral Care of Homosexual Persons*, 17.

[153] *Gravissimum Educationis*, 1.

[154] *Familiaris Consortio*, 37.

[155] For example: (*a*) visual erotic material, (*b*) written or verbal erotic presentations (cf. *Educational Guidance in Human Love*, 76), (*c*) obscene or coarse language, (*d*) indecent humour, (*e*) the denigration of chastity and (*f*) attempts to minimize the gravity of sin against this virtue.

This *principle of respect for the child* excludes all improper forms of involving children and young people. In this regard, among other things, this can include the following *methods that abuse sex education*: (*a*) every "dramatized" representation, mime or "role playing" which depict genital or erotic matters, (*b*) making drawings, charts or models etc. of this nature, (*c*) seeking personal information about sexual questions[156] or asking that family information be divulged, (*d*) oral or written exams about genital or erotic questions.

Particular Methods

128.   Parents and all who help them should keep these principles and norms in mind when they take up various methods which seem suitable in the light of parental and expert experience. We will now go on to single out these recommended methods. The main methods to avoid will also be indicated, together with the ideologies that promote and inspire them.

Recommended Methods

129.   The normal and fundamental method, already proposed in this guide, is *personal dialogue between parents and their children,* that is, *individual formation within the family circle.* In fact there is no substitute for a dialogue of trust and openness between parents and their children, a dialogue which respects not only their stages of development but also the young persons as individuals. However, when parents seek help from others, there are various useful methods which can be recommended in the light of parental experience and in conformity with Christian prudence.

130. 1. As couples or as individuals, parents can *meet with others who are prepared for education for love* to draw on their experience and competence. These people can offer explanations and provide parents with books and other resources approved by the ecclesiastical authorities.

131. 2. Parents who are not always prepared to face up to the problematic side of education for love can take part in meetings with their children, guided by expert persons who are worthy of trust, for example, doctors, priests, educators. In some cases, in the interest of greater freedom of expression, meetings where only daughters or sons are present seem preferable.

---

[156] Excluding the context of prudent and appropriate teaching about the natural regulation of fertility.

132. 3. In certain situations, parents can *entrust part of education for love to another trustworthy person,* if there are matters which require a specific competence or pastoral care in particular cases.

133. 4. *Catechesis on morality* may be provided by other trustworthy persons, with particular emphasis on sexual ethics at puberty and adolescence. Parents should take an interest in the moral catechesis which is given to their own children outside the home and use it as a support for their own educational work. Such catechesis must not include the more intimate aspects of sexual information, whether biological or affective, which belong to individual formation within the family.[157]

134. 5. The *religious formation of the parents themselves,* in particular solid catechetical preparation of adults in the truth of love, builds the foundations of a mature faith that can guide them in the formation of their own children.[158] This adult catechesis enables them not only to deepen their understanding of the community of life and love in marriage, but also helps them learn how to communicate better with their own children. Furthermore, in the very process of forming their children in love, parents will find that they benefit much, because they will discover that this ministry of love helps them to "maintain a living awareness of the 'gift' they continually receive from their children".[159] To make parents capable of carrying out their educational work, special formation courses with the help of experts can be promoted.

Methods and Ideologies to Avoid

135. Today parents should be attentive to ways in which an immoral education can be passed on to their children through various methods promoted by groups with positions and interests contrary to Christian morality.[160] It would be impossible to indicate all unacceptable methods. Here are presented only some of the more widely diffused methods that threaten the rights of parents and the moral life of their children.

136. In the first place, parents must reject *secularized and anti-natalist sex education,* which puts God at the margin of life and regards the birth of a child as a threat. This sex education is spread by large organizations and international associations that promote abortion, sterilization and contraception. These organizations want to impose a false lifestyle against the truth of human sexuality. Working at national or state levels,

[157] Cf. *Educational Guidance in Human Love,* 58.
[158] Cf. *Ibid.,* 63.
[159] *Familiaris Consortio,* 21.
[160] Cf. Letter to Families, *Gratissimam Sane,* 13.

these organizations try to arouse the fear of the "threat of over-population" among children and young people to promote the contraceptive mentality, that is, the "anti-life" mentality. They spread false ideas about the "reproductive health" and "sexual and reproductive rights" of young people.[161] Furthermore, some antinatalist organizations maintain those clinics which, violating the rights of parents, provide abortion and contraception for young people, thus promoting promiscuity and consequently an increase in teenage pregnancies. "As we look towards the year 2000, how can we fail to think of the young? What is being held up to them? A society of 'things' and not of 'persons'. The right to do as they will from their earliest years, without any constraint, provided it is 'safe'. The unreserved gift of self, mastery of one's instincts, the sense of responsibility — these are notions considered as belonging to another age".[162]

137.   Before adolescence, the immoral nature of *abortion,* surgical or chemical, can be gradually explained in terms of Catholic morality and reverence for human life.[163]

As regards *sterilization and contraception,* these should not be discussed before adolescence and only in conformity with the teaching of the Catholic Church.[164] Therefore, the moral, spiritual and health values of methods for the natural regulation of fertility will be emphasized, at the same time indicating the dangers and ethical aspects of the artificial methods. In particular, the substantial and deep difference between natural methods and artificial methods will be shown, both with regard to respect for God's plan for marriage as well as for achieving "the total reciprocal self-giving of husband and wife"[165] and openness to life.

138.   In some societies professional associations of *sex-educators, sex-counsellors and sex-therapists* are operating. Because their work is often based on unsound theories, lacking scientific value and closed to an authentic anthropology, and theories that do not recognize the true value of chastity, parents should regard such associations with great caution, no matter what official recognition they may have received. When their outlook is out of harmony with the teachings of the Church, this is evident not only in their work, but also in their publications which are widely diffused in various countries.

139.   Another abuse occurs whenever *sex education* is given to children by teaching them all the intimate details of genital relationships, even in a graphic way. Today

[161] Cf. Pontifical Council for the Family, "Instrumentum laboris", *Ethical and Pastoral Dimensions of Population Trends,* Libreria Editrice Vaticana, March 25, 1994, 23 and 84; *Educational Guidance in Human Love,* 62.
[162] *Letter of the Holy Father to the Heads of State* in view of the Cairo Conference, March 19, 1994; *L'Osservatore Romano,* English edition, April 20, 1994, p. 1.
[163] Cf. *Evangelium Vitae,* 58-63.
[164] Cf. *Educational Guidance in Human Love,* 62.
[165] *Familiaris Consortio,* 32.

this is often motivated by wanting to provide education for "safe sex", above all in relation to the spread of AIDS. In this situation, parents must also reject the promotion of so-called "safe sex" or "safer sex", a dangerous and immoral policy based on the deluded theory that the condom can provide adequate protection against AIDS. Parents must insist on continence outside marriage and fidelity in marriage as the only true and secure education for the prevention of this contagious disease.

140.   One widely-used, but possibly harmful, approach goes by the name of "values clarification". Young people are encouraged to reflect upon, to clarify and to decide upon moral issues with the greatest degree of "autonomy", ignoring the objective reality of the moral law in general and disregarding the formation of consciences on the specific Christian moral precepts, as affirmed by the Magisterium of the Church.[166] Young people are given the idea that a moral code is something which they create themselves, as if man were the source and norm of morality.

However, the values clarification method impedes the true freedom and autonomy of young people at an insecure stage of their development.[167] In practice, not only is the opinion of the majority favoured, but complex moral situations are put before young people, far removed from the normal moral choices they face each day, in which good or evil are easily recognizable. This unacceptable method tends to be closely linked with moral relativism, and thus encourages indifference to moral law and permissiveness.

141.   Parents should also be attentive to ways in which sexual instruction can be inserted in the context of other subjects which are otherwise useful (for example, health and hygiene, personal development, family life, children's literature, social and cultural studies etc.). In these situations it is more difficult to control the content of sexual instruction. This *method of inclusion* is used in particular by those who promote sex instruction within the perspective of birth control or in countries where the government does not respect the rights of parents in this field. But catechesis would also be distorted if the inseparable links between religion and morality were to be used as a pretext for introducing into religious instruction the biological and affective sexual information which the parents should give according to their prudent decision in their own home.[168]

142.   Finally, as a general guideline, one needs to bear in mind, that all the different methods of sexual education should be judged by parents in the light of the princi-

---

[166] Cf. John Paul II, Encyclical Letter, *Veritatis Splendor*, August 6, 1993, 95-97; *AAS* 85 (1993), pp. 1208-1210.

[167] Cf. *Ibid.*, 41, on man's true moral autonomy.

[168] Cf. *Educational Guidance in Human Love*, 58.

ples and moral norms of the Church, which express human values in daily life.[169] The negative effects which various methods can produce in the personality of children and young people should also be taken into account.

Inculturation and Education for Love

143.   An authentic education for love must take account of the cultural context in which the parents and their children live. As a union between professed faith and concrete life, inculturization means creating a harmonious relationship between faith and culture, where Christ and his Gospel have absolute precedence over culture. "Therefore, because it transcends the entire natural and cultural order, the Christian faith is, on the one hand, compatible with all cultures insofar as they conform to right reason and good will, and, on the other hand, to an eminent degree, is a dynamizing factor of culture. A single principle explains the totality of relationships between faith and culture: Grace respects nature, healing in it the wounds of sin, comforting and elevating it. Elevation to the divine life is the specific finality of grace, but it cannot realize this unless nature is healed and unless elevation to the supernatural order brings nature, in the way proper to itself, to the plenitude of perfection".[170] Therefore, explicit and premature sex education can never be justified in the name of a prevailing secularized culture. On the contrary, parents must educate their own children to understand and face up to the forces of this culture, so that they may always follow the way of Christ.

144.   In traditional cultures, parents must not accept practices which are contrary to Christian morality, for example rites associated with puberty which sometimes involve introducing young people to sexual practices or acts contrary to the dignity and rights of the person, such as the genital mutilation of girls. Thus the authorities of the Church are to judge whether local customs are compatible with Christian morality. But, the traditions of modesty and reserve in sexual matters, which characterize various societies, must be respected everywhere. At the same time, the right of young people to adequate information must be maintained. Furthermore, the particular role of the family in such a culture must be respected,[171] without imposing any Western model of sex education.

---

[169] Cf. *Ibid.,* 19; *Familiaris Consortio,* 37.
[170] International Theological Commission, *Faith and Inculturization,* I, 10, October 3-8, 1988.
[171] Cf. *Familiaris Consortio,* 66.

VIII

CONCLUSION

Assistance for Parents

145.   There are various way of helping and supporting parents in fulfilling their fundamental right and duty to educate their children for love. Such assistance never means taking from parents or diminishing their formative right and duty, because they remain "original and primary", "irreplaceable and inalienable".[172] Therefore, the role which others can carry out in helping parents is always (*a*) *subsidiary,* because the formative role of the family is always preferable, and (*b*) *subordinate,* that is, subject to the parents' attentive guidance and control. Everyone must observe the right order of cooperation and collaboration between parents and those who can help them in their task. It is clear that the assistance of others must be given first and foremost to parents rather than to their children.

146.   Those who are called to help parents in educating their children for love must be disposed and prepared to teach in conformity with the authentic moral doctrine of the Catholic Church. Moreover, they must be mature persons, of a good moral reputation, faithful to their own Christian state of life, married or single, laity, religious or priests. They must not only be prepared in the details of moral and sexual information but they must also be sensitive to the rights and role of parents and the family, as well as the needs and problems of children and young people.[173] In this way, in the light of the principles and content of this guide, they must enter "into the same spirit that animates parents".[174] But if parents believe themselves to be capable of providing an adequate education for love, they are not bound to accept assistance.

Valid Sources for Education for Love

147.   The Pontifical Council for the Family is aware of the great need for valid material, specifically prepared for parents in conformity with the principles set out in

---

[172] Cf. *Familiaris Consortio,* 36 and 40; Letter to Families, *Gratissimam Sane,* 16.

[173] Those who help parents can adapt the principles indicated for teachers in *Educational Guidance in Human Love,* 79-89.

[174] *Familiaris Consortio,* 37.

this guide. Parents who are competent in this field and convinced of these principles should be involved in preparing this material. They will thus be able to offer their own experience and wisdom in order to help others educate their children for chastity. Parents will also welcome the assistance and supervision of the appropriate ecclesiastical authorities in promoting suitable material and in removing or correcting what does not conform to the principles set out in this guide, concerning doctrine, timing and the content and method of such education.[175] These principles also apply to all the modern means of social communication. In a special way, this Pontifical Council for the Family is counting on the work of sensitization and support by the Episcopal Conferences, who will know how to vindicate, where necessary, the right of the family and parents and their proper domains, also with regard to State educational programmes.

Solidarity with Parents

148.   In fulfilling a ministry of love to their own children, parents should enjoy the support and cooperation of the other members of the Church. The *rights* of parents must be recognized, protected and maintained, not only to ensure solid formation of children and young people, but also to guarantee the right order of cooperation and collaboration between parents and those who can help them in their task. Likewise, in parishes or apostolates, clergy and religious should support and encourage parents in striving to form their own children. In their turn, parents should remember that the family is not the only or exclusive formative community. Thus they should cultivate a cordial and active relationship with other persons who can help them, while never forgetting their own inalienable rights.

Hope and Trust

149.   In the face of many challenges to Christian chastity, the gifts of nature and grace which parents enjoy always remain the most solid foundations on which the Church forms her children. *Much of the formation in the home is indirect,* incarnated in a loving and tender atmosphere, for it arises from the presence and example of parents whose love is pure and generous. If parents are given confidence in this task of education for love, they will be inspired to overcome the challenges and problems of our times by their own ministry of love.

150.   The Pontifical Council for the Family therefore urges parents to have confidence in their rights and duties regarding the education of their children, so as to go forward with wisdom and knowledge, knowing that they are sustained by God's gift.

[175] See above, nos. 65-76, 121-144.

In this noble task, may parents always place their trust in God through prayer to the Holy Spirit, the gentle Paraclete and Giver of all good gifts. May they seek the powerful intercession and protection of Mary Immaculate, the Virgin Mother of fair love and model of faithful purity. Let them also invoke Saint Joseph, her just and chaste spouse, following his example of fidelity and purity of heart.[176] May parents constantly rely on the love which they offer to their own children, a love which "casts out fear", which "bears all things, believes all things, hopes all things, endures all things" (*1 Corinthians* 13:7). Such love is and must be aimed towards eternity, towards the unending happiness promised by Our Lord Jesus Christ to those who follow him: "Blessed are the pure of heart, for they shall see God" (*Matthew* 5:8).

Vatican City, December 8, 1995

ALFONSO Card. LÓPEZ TRUJILLO
*President of the Pontifical Council
for the Family*

✠ Most Rev. ELIO SGRECCIA
*Titular Bishop of Zama Minor
Secretary of the Pontifical Council
for the Family*

---

[176] Cf. John Paul II, Apostolic Exhortation, *Redemptoris Custos,* August 15, 1990, 31; *AAS* 82 (1990), p. 33.